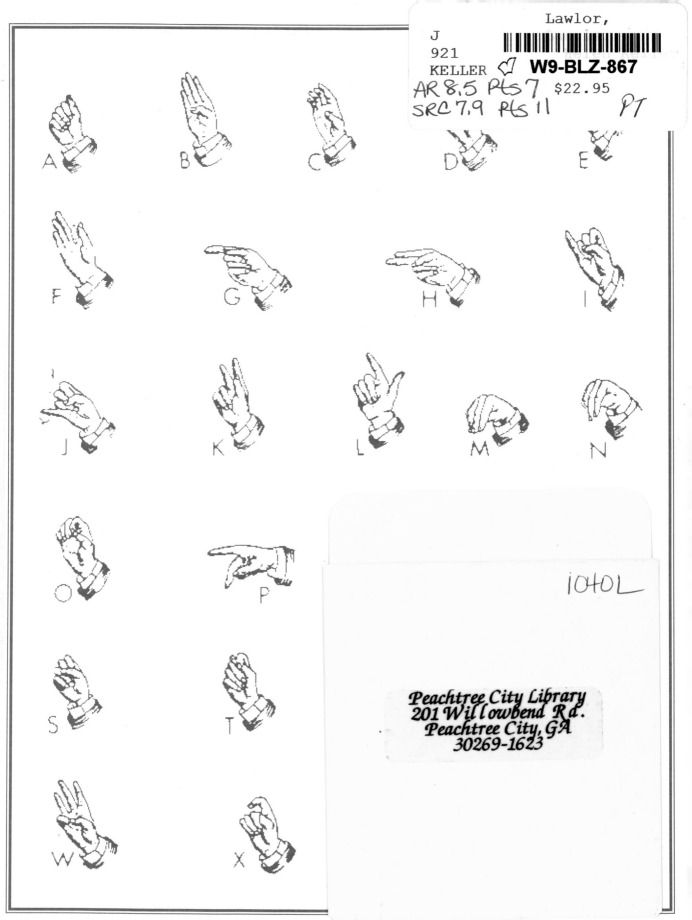

Helen Keller

Rebellious Spirit

Helen Keller

Rebellious Spirit

LAURIE LAWLOR

Holiday House / New York

For Bodhi

Photo Credits
The prints and photographs in this book are
from the following sources and used by permission:

Courtesy of the Perkins School for the Blind: pages *i, ii,* 1, 28, 31, 38, 43, 46, 52, 53, 54,
57, 59, 77, 84, 87, 90, 112, 123, 132, 144, 154, 157

Courtesy of the American Federation for the Blind: pages *viii,* 6, 9, 26, 64, 68, 89, 91, 93,
96, 100, 108, 111, 130, 133, 136, 138, 143, 145, 150

Courtesy of the Library of Congress: pages 3, 24, 29, 30, 69, 71, 74, 103, 107, 120, 126, 148

Photographs by Larry Gillentine © 1995: pages 10, 11, 16, 20, 21, 35, 36, 37, 42

Courtesy of the Alabama State Historical Archives: pages 14, 22

Courtesy of the Landrum Collection: pages 15, 40

Courtesy of The Hadley School for the Blind: page 50

From *Helen Keller Souvenir,* No. 2, 1899: Volta
Bureau, Washington, D.C.: pages 80, 86

Library of Congress Cataloging-in-Publication Data
Lawlor, Laurie.
Helen Keller: rebellious spirit / by Laurie Lawlor.
p.   cm.
Includes bibliographical references and index.
ISBN 0-8234-1588-0 (hardcover)
1. Keller, Helen, 1880–1968—Juvenile literature.
2. Blind-deaf women—United States—Biography—
Juvenile literature. 3. Blind-deaf women—
Education—United States—Juvenile literature.
[1. Keller, Helen, 1880–1968.
2. Blind. 3. Deaf.
4. Physically handicapped.
5. Women—Biography.] I. Title.
HV1624.K4 L39 2001
362.4'1'092—dc21
[B] 00-036950

Contents

Introduction   *1*

1. Along the Rolling Tennessee River   *7*

2. Nothing Would Ever Be the Same Again   *17*

3. The Big Breakthrough   *27*

4. So Much to Ask About   *39*

5. No Ordinary Child   *47*

6. An Unexpected Shift in the Wind   *55*

7. A Widening Circle of Experience   *65*

8. A Dream and a Challenge   *75*

9. "To Be Myself"   *85*

10. Breaking New Ground   *97*

11. On Stage   *109*

12. Love and Exile   *121*

13. Bright Lights of Hollywood and Vaudeville   *131*

14. A New Career   *139*

15. "Someone Who Liked to Laugh"   *149*

Epilogue   *153*

Chronology   158

Source Notes   160

For Further Reading   161

Index   166

The only lightless dark

is the night

of ignorance and

insensibility.

　　　—Helen Keller,

　　　　The World I Live In

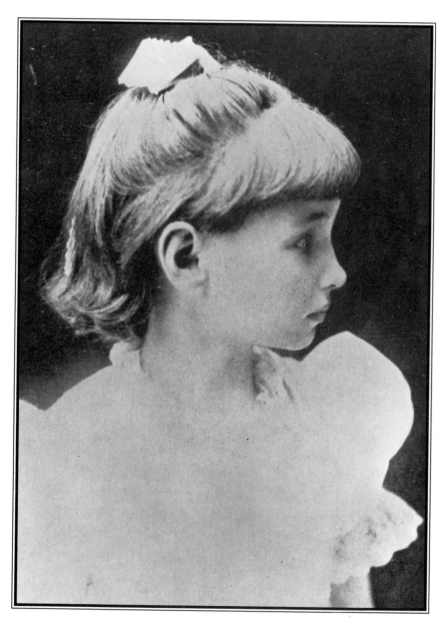

Earliest surviving photo of Helen, taken August 1, 1887,
in Tuscumbia. Helen was seven years old.

Introduction

HELEN KELLER NEVER FORGOT the delight she felt on May 26, 1888, the day she communicated freely and directly with children her own age for the first time in her life.

She was nearly eight years old. Both blind and deaf, she had made the long, hot journey by train with her teacher from the Keller home in Tuscumbia, Alabama, to Perkins Institution for the Blind in Boston. The moment Helen arrived seemed to her to be "a beautiful fairy tale come true." After writing eager letters to the blind students at Perkins during the past year, she was finally going to meet them in person.

As soon as Helen stepped from the carriage outside the impressive five-story building, the boys and girls hurried down the front steps to greet her. They surrounded her and swiftly spelled their names, jokes, and gossip into the palm of her outstretched, cupped right hand. Helen was as fluent as the students who used the one-hand manual alphabet—a series of twenty-six different finger positions representing different letters.

Perkins Institution for the Blind in Boston as it looked when Helen arrived in 1888.

For once Helen was not an outsider. For once she had no need for a grown-up to translate for her. She could speak directly without worrying that someone would correct or censor her conversation. "What joy to talk with other children in my own language!" she later wrote. "Until then I had been like a foreigner speaking through an interpreter."

Helen's direct connection with Perkins, a place she once described as "her own country," only lasted until 1892. From that point on, she had to make her way in the hearing and sighted world where few people spoke or understood her special language. Her struggle to be seen and heard as a whole and capable human being would both confound and challenge her for the rest of her life.

Helen lost her ability to hear, see, and talk when she was nineteen months old. In 1887, at age seven, she was pronounced a "miracle" when a Boston newspaper exaggerated a report that she had overcome all her handicaps and could communicate, read—even sing—thanks to the help of a dedicated teacher. Over the years publicity would transform the attractive prodigy, who was called everything from "angel-child" to "Eighth Wonder of the World," into a compelling, modern "New Woman," a twentieth-century Saint Joan of Arc who defied all odds by graduating from Radcliffe College, becoming a best-selling author and lecturer, and traveling to every corner of the world to promote the welfare of the blind, deaf, and poor.

Her remarkable life was celebrated in countless articles, books, documentaries, and photographs. She was the subject of an Academy Award–winning film and a long-running Broadway hit. She received countless honors, from the Chevalier of the French Legion of Honor to the Presidential Medal of Freedom. She personally met with every president from Grover Cleveland to John F. Kennedy. Among her friends were such famous individuals as Mark Twain, Alexander Graham Bell, and Eleanor Roosevelt.

And yet, although thousands of people recognized Helen Keller's name, had seen her picture, or marveled at her accomplishments, few could imagine what it was like to be blind and deaf. Fewer still could imag-

Helen managed to coax a smile from ordinarily serious President Calvin Coolidge during a visit in 1926.

ine Helen Keller as a fully complete human being—not just a famous, smiling plaster saint.

Helen Keller worked very hard to maintain an image of loving goodness and inexhaustible happiness. She struggled with incredible determination for years to try to speak so that others could easily understand her. She painstakingly created works of fiction and nonfiction that she hoped the sighted and the hearing would read and comprehend.

Always gregarious, she became adept in the small talk, manners, and niceties of social gatherings—when to laugh, how to focus her attention toward a speaker, how to use the right fork and never spill anything at a formal dinner. She wore attractive, stylish clothing that she couldn't see and often had to patiently endure dialogue and the to-and-fro of argument between two or more people she couldn't lip-read. Surrounded almost constantly by the hearing, she never became part of a deaf community—people who communicated through sign language and enjoyed regular, easy companionship.

"The experience of the deaf-blind person, in a world of seeing, hearing people, is like that of a sailor on an island where the inhabitants speak a language unknown to him, whose life is unlike that he has lived," Helen wrote. "He is one, they are many; there is no chance of compromise. He must learn to see with their eyes, to hear with their ears, to think their thoughts, to follow their ideals." Like that shipwrecked sailor, she lived as an outsider in a world that demanded that to be accepted as "normal" one must be able to see and hear and speak—or at least appear to do so.

Although her success depended on how well she could conform outwardly and be like everyone else as much as she could, she eventually learned that to live in harmony with herself and the world she had to preserve her own sense of inner identity. To do this she cultivated a quiet, stubborn persistence, audacity, defiance—even rebelliousness. Her unique spiritual views and strong opinions on topics rang-

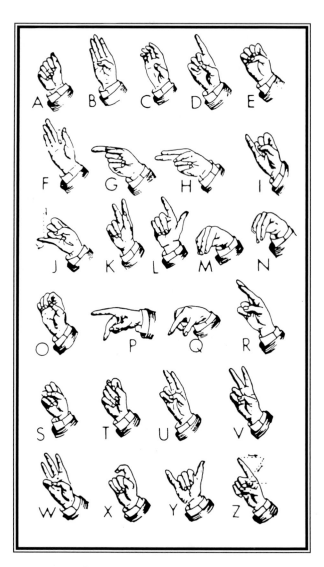

Manual alphabet used by Helen

ing from women's rights to vote and to birth control to integration and socialism would have shocked the people of her time who thought of her only as a nonthreatening, admirable icon.

Helen Keller's life was seldom dull. Even ordinariness, which most of us take for granted—opening the front door with our own key, walking down the street, buying a hot dog at a hot-dog stand—couldn't be achieved by her without great effort. Undoubtedly she would have agreed with David Wright, a deaf poet who wrote, "The disabled have been given a built-in, ready-packed objective which is always present: a definite impediment to get the better of."

Helen Keller never thought of her constant struggle as particularly heroic. She never considered herself unusually gifted. Like so many disabled people, she did what she had to in order to survive. In return, she wanted no pity—she only wanted to be treated like anyone else. Her challenge was the same one we all face: to know ourselves and to make ourselves known. She managed to do this with a sense of humor and remarkable energy—something almost everyone who ever met her commented on.

Poet Carl Sandburg saw Helen Keller onstage at the Palace Theater in New York City in 1922. He wrote to tell her how surprised he was to find her "something of a dancer, shifting in easy postures like a good-blooded racehorse." But it was the reaction of the crowd he found most fascinating: "It was interesting to watch that audience minute by minute come along till they loved you big and far," he wrote. "Possibly the finest thing about your performance is that those who hear and see you feel that zest for living, the zest you radiate, is more important than any formula about how to live life."

*Helen aboard ship near the Orkney Islands of Scotland
in 1932. "I am especially alive to the spell of the sea,"
she wrote in* Midstream.

1.
Along the Rolling Tennessee River

My hands evoke sight and sound out of feeling, inter-shifting the senses endlessly; linking motion with sight, odor with sound. . . .

—Helen Keller, "A Chant of Darkness,"
The World I Live In

ALL HER LIFE THE ONE PLACE Helen Keller felt particularly at home was the ocean. A strong swimmer, she was fearless in high surf at the beach or aboard any kind of boat in any kind of weather, even bad storms.

In 1930, while her lifelong teacher, companion, and guide Annie Sullivan Macy wept and moaned with seasickness on an especially rough steamship passage from America to England, fifty-year-old Helen eagerly made her way around careening trunks and rolling oranges and apples in their cabin and climbed up on deck to face the biting wind and spray. It's not surprising that when she turned eighty, spry Helen insisted on going for a dip in the Atlantic over the protests of her horrified, staid, seventy-five-year-old sister Mildred.

"I could never stay long enough at the shore," Helen wrote in her autobiography, *The Story of My Life*.

To understand Helen Keller's sensory world, what better place to begin than her first visit to the ocean?

It was a bright summer day in 1888 at the beach in Cape Cod, Massachusetts. Helen had just turned eight. She wore flannel drawers and a tunic, the fashionable bathing costume of young girls. Sturdy, tall, and athletic, she had light brown shoulder-length curls. Other beachgoers might have guessed she was blind only if they noticed the cloudiness of her pale blue eyes or the way her left eye protruded slightly.

Of course, Helen was too busy to care what anyone thought of her appearance. Impatiently, she scrambled away from her teacher and hurried toward the water. Something of a bookworm, she had just finished reading about the ocean in a book in Braille, with its special raised dot lettering. More than anything she wanted to touch what she called "the mighty sea."

Sun warmed the top of Helen's head. Wind tangled her hair. She could neither see the vast ocean nor hear the waves, yet she sensed the water's enormous presence. With outstretched arms she sniffed the fresh breeze that smelled of great open distance. The soft ground shifted beneath her bare feet. Anyone watching her that day might have seen her walk crooked-crazy, laugh, fall to her knees, and clutch a handful of sand that felt fine as sugar. Did it taste as sweet? Always a great experimenter, she undoubtedly licked her hand, then spit the sand that tasted as bitter as wallpaper and grainy as brick.

For a moment, she rested on her hands and knees. Although she could not see the other beachgoers, she must have felt the ground shake and tremble through her calves and up through her arms. *Thump whump thump whump*—the unmistakable rumbling of footsteps hurrying past. And farther away, faint and rhythmic as a great heartbeat, she was aware of a strange, powerful booming. She stood and hurried closer.

Wind spattered spray. Droplets clung to her skin. She sniffed again. The smell changed and became a mixture of odors—the scent of just-born puppies, soggy wood, and green fruit ripening. Waves rumbled against her ankles. The current swirled and sucked her feet into the heavy wet sand. Fearlessly, she plunged forward into the cool water. "I felt the great billows rock and sink," she remembered. "The buoyant motion of the water filled me with an exquisite, quivering joy."

Her pleasure ended when she accidentally bumped her foot on a rock and lost her balance. She could not see the approach of an enormous wave that arched and crashed overhead. She tumbled upside down. Dizzy and choking, she flailed her arms. Before she could right herself, another wave flattened her again. Solid ground vanished. She clutched handfuls of seaweed and sand. Which way was up? Her lungs must have felt as if they might burst. Suddenly, the water heaved and bucked her into the shallows.

Sputtering and gasping for breath, she crawled to dry land. Her soggy hair lay plastered over her eyes. Sand clogged her ears and nostrils. Her mouth puckered with a terrible taste.

With relief she felt the unexpected embrace of her worried teacher. But as soon as undaunted Helen caught her breath, she demanded angrily, "Who put salt in the water?"

Helen began her life far away from any ocean. She was born June 27, 1880, in the sleepy little town of Tuscumbia in northwestern Alabama. The nearest body of water was the Tennessee River, which flowed wide and crooked and occasionally dull brown-red when rain washed down soil from the surrounding low hills.

As an infant Helen could see and hear perfectly. Her parents, forty-three-year-old Captain Arthur H. Keller and Kate Adams Keller, nearly

Kate Adams Keller, Helen's mother   *Captain Arthur H. Keller, Helen's father*

Helen was born June 27, 1880, in this bedroom in the Little House.
The cradle in the foreground was used by Helen as a baby.
The white sewing basket belonged to her mother.

twenty years his junior, were thrilled with their bright and eager newborn daughter. By the age of six months, Helen amazed and delighted everyone by calling, "How d'ye" and "tea, tea, tea." When Helen was a year old, she took her first steps. Her proud mother recalled how her curious little daughter escaped from her arms after a bath and trotted away to investigate a pool of sunlight dancing on the floor through an open door. Her mother bragged how cleverly Helen spotted needles and buttons on the floor no one else could find.

Adored, golden-curled Helen was Kate Adams Keller's first baby. Tall, statuesque, and blond, Kate was sensitive and intelligent. She was a voracious reader with a remarkable memory. Once upon a time she had been a pampered Memphis belle who knew nothing about running a plantation or a large household staffed by many black servants. She was said to have married Captain Keller in a fit of anger over another suitor. She may have regretted her hasty decision. After only a few months of marriage, she went for days without speaking to her husband.

Adhering to the proper Victorian southern woman's adage, "Suffer and be still," Kate knew it was not seemly or Christian to complain about her situation. Her place now was in the home, and that was where she directed all her energy. She threw herself into her new job as a tireless, devoted housekeeper and mother. With great effort, she learned to cook. She canned her own preserves, cured her own hams, made her own soap, and oversaw the vegetable and flower gardens.

Kate was Captain Keller's second wife. Their marriage had taken place in 1878, just a year after the death of his first wife, Sarah. Captain Keller's two sons from his first marriage, twenty-two-year-old James and fifteen-year-old Simpson, doubtless welcomed their new baby sister with more enthusiasm than they had welcomed Kate Adams, their moody new mother.

Ivy Green, the family home, was a comfortable white clapboard house covered with English ivy. Surrounded by fragrant boxwood, mimosa, and magnolia trees, Ivy Green was part of a 640-acre tract plantation that included Helen's birthplace, the nearby "Little House." Helen fondly recalled this smaller structure with one large room, a bay window, and a porch covered with sweet-smelling roses and "masses of tangled honey-suckle and paulownia blossoms heavy in the afternoon heat."

In Tuscumbia, a town with less than two thousand inhabitants, every-one knew the Kellers. A half-dozen aunts, uncles, or cousins might be found at any barbecue, old-time fiddle dance, or all-day singing and "din-ner on the grounds" at the church. Captain Keller ran the local newspaper,

Helen met Annie for the first time on the front porch of her family's home,
Ivy Green. The Little House is on the far right.

The North Alabamian, when he wasn't running for political office or hunting with his numerous beloved dogs. "His hospitality was great, almost to a fault," Helen remembered, "and he seldom came home without bringing a guest."

Nothing pleased Captain Keller more than a chance to entertain dinner company with colorful stories about his days as an officer at the siege of Vicksburg during the War Between the States (known in the northern states as the Civil War). Although Confederate General Robert E. Lee had surrendered in April 1865, the grown-ups Helen knew as a young child sometimes seemed to act as if the war had never ended. The traumatic event still dominated the lives and conversations of the people of Tuscumbia. They pointed with bitterness at houses where Yankee bullets remained lodged in the walls. They knew exactly which pile of bricks marked the chimney of a once gracious mansion burned to the ground by Yankee invaders. They told one another of recurring nightmares filled with the terrifying cries of house slaves calling, "The Yankees are coming!" One elderly woman from Tuscumbia recalled to the end of her days the sounds of clanking sabers, wailing blue-coated cavalrymen, and the *chink-chink-chink* of enemy spurs dragging on her family's polished parlor floor.

Helen grew up around people resentful of the suffering they had experienced and the fact that their former way of life seemed to be gone forever. Throughout her early childhood, Tuscumbia, like so many other small southern towns, had not yet recovered from the Civil War or the Reconstruction that followed. Nearly 100,000 men and boys from Alabama had marched away to fight for the Confederacy. Only 30,000 returned. Every family had been touched by death or disease or crippling. When the war ended, the region was economically depressed and politically disorganized. Farmers plowed among corpses. Homeless families hid in makeshift hovels and searched battlefields for old bullets to sell as scrap metal.

Captain Keller, like so many others, lost his fortune when his family's land became worthless. Throughout the South, taxes skyrocketed. The South owed $712 million in war debts to the U.S. government. Meanwhile it would take untold millions of dollars to replace destroyed livestock, crops, railroads, and roads.

The most destitute of all, however, were former slaves. They numbered 435,000—more than half the total Alabama population. The slaves had been freed but most had no skills. Few could read. They had no work, no money, and nowhere to go. To survive economically, many blacks became sharecroppers and worked on their former owners' land. Most of the black children Helen knew when she was growing up lived and worked on her father's cotton plantation or helped out in her parents' house. Like so many other freed slaves, the children's parents had taken up small plots of ground on which they planted and "chopped," or hoed, cotton. In exchange they provided their landlord with part of their crop in payment. Sharecroppers often had to buy overpriced food, seeds, and supplies in local stores on credit.

Reconstruction, a federal plan organized by the North to rebuild the South, assumed responsibility for Alabama's government, courts, and schools. Not surprisingly, southerners deeply resented this Yankee inter-ference. People in Tuscumbia and other small towns paid a high price for Reconstruction's failure. It would not be until 1877, only three years before Helen was born, that the last of the 200,000 federal troops finally pulled out of the South and ended more than twelve years of occupation.

Although freed slaves in Tuscumbia and elsewhere had been able to take advantage of free schooling and training offered by Reconstruction's local Freedman's Bureaus, these ended as soon as the last Yankee went home. Southern states rewrote their constitutions. Freed blacks were reduced to a condition of economic dependency and social degradation. They were systematically barred from voting by complicated election-day laws that required special "poll taxes." Their children were forbidden to go to church or school with white children. Throughout the 1880s masked and hooded riders of the Ku Klux Klan terrorized black families, lynched black men, and burned farms in Colbert County and elsewhere in Alabama to terrify the black population back into submission.

Helen's father's newspaper, *The North Alabamian*, did not officially cover stories of local Klan lynchings. However, Captain Keller did not dis-guise his own racial sentiments when he reported "an exciting chase" in early January 1882, when a large posse of citizens, a pack of dogs, and the sheriff ran through Tuscumbia's yards and gardens in pursuit of "a negro from Russellville." Like so many individuals of his time, place, and social standing, Captain Keller did not believe that Negroes were human beings. His lifelong prejudice, however, was something his daughter would never embrace.

Captain Keller and the readers of *The North Alabamian* were undoubtedly aware of the poverty experienced not only by blacks but by whites as well. Numerous large poor white families crowded into one-room shacks hidden among the hills outside Tuscumbia. These rented houses were without glass or screens in the windows to keep out the wind or the mosquitoes. In cold weather the only ventilation for smoky wood-burning stoves were cracks in the ceiling. White sharecroppers ate corn bread, bacon, and syrup and could afford wheat flour biscuits only one day a week. Their children went barefoot and caught hookworm or "toe itch" and became anemic and lethargic from their poor diet. White children who were younger than age fourteen eagerly took jobs working twelve-hour days in northern Alabama textile mills and mines for the privilege of earning a few dollars a week. Their employers refused to hire black children.

While the rest of America bustled with booming cities, reckless industrial growth, and a population that topped fifty million for the first time, Tuscumbia and the rest of the South in 1880 were experiencing a struggling economy, stagnant population, and, for many, appalling social con-

Captain Keller's weekly newspaper, The North Alabamian, *featured as its motto: "Here shall the press the People's rights maintain, unawed by influence, unbribed by gain."*

*Ox carts were not uncommon on the unpaved main street
of Tuscumbia when Helen was growing up.*

ditions. The per capita income in the North was $1,353; in the South it
was less than $376.

For both the poor and the better-off citizens of Tuscumbia, the pace of
life was slow and predictable. During Helen's early childhood, few innova-
tions and fewer strangers came to town. There was no public library, no
theater, no electric lights. Between 1890 and 1900 the population of
Tuscumbia actually dropped from 2,491 to 2,348.

Although Helen's family had lost most of their fortune during the war,
were forced to pay high taxes, and had trouble finding banks that would
lend them money, they were not destitute. Both Helen's mother and
father were well-read and owned many books. Her two older half brothers
were educated privately. The Kellers, like other white upper-middle-class
Tuscumbia residents, were simply "land poor." They owned property but
never had much cash on hand. What was more important in a tight-knit
community like Tuscumbia was the Kellers' long-standing reputation.

They seemed to be the lucky, favored family.

That is, until one day in February 1882, when nineteen-month-old
Helen became ill.

As the first child of doting parents, Helen was given numerous toys.
Many of her playthings are preserved in the playroom of the Little House,
the small house near Ivy Green.

2.

Nothing Would Ever Be the Same Again

I cannot remember how I felt when the light went out of my eyes. I suppose I thought it was always night, and perhaps I wondered why day did not come.
—Handwritten reminiscence of Helen's earliest childhood, recorded by Annie Sullivan

*I*N AN AGE when antibiotics did not exist, desperate parents in the Tennessee River Valley used any folk cure they could find to prevent or cure their children's illnesses. No one knew when the next deadly outbreak of yellow fever or diphtheria would strike. One folk cure recommended tying bags of bitter-smelling asafetida around a child's neck to ward off whooping cough. Another claimed that tea brewed with nine dead sowbugs cured rashes inside a baby's mouth.

When Helen came down with a high fever, the Kellers sent for the local doctor. He pronounced her condition "acute congestion of the stomach and the brain," a name given to any mysterious illness with no known cause or cure. He said she wouldn't live. For days Helen's frantic mother and father hovered over her.

And then one morning, Helen's fever vanished. Her family rejoiced. No one knew that she had become completely deaf. After a few days, Helen began to lose her sight as well. Helen's memories of this time were sketchy at best. She later recalled lying in somebody's lap. "And suddenly I was raised in a bright light. I felt a great pain which made me scream violently."

Like many children younger than age two who lose their sight and hearing, Helen could not recall what the loss felt like. She adapted quickly to her new situation and did not feel the sadness or remorse an older person might experience.

Her parents, however, were not to be consoled. What would happen to their precious daughter now? What would become of her? There would be no flocks of eager suitors, no cotillion parties, no handsome rich husband. "Fear ambushed the joy in my heart when I was twenty-four and left me for dead," Kate Adams Keller wrote when she found out that her daughter was blind and deaf. One friend recalled how lines of sorrow became etched around Kate's sensitive mouth. A brittle, withdrawn attitude of mourning came over her and colored her relationship not only with Helen but with everyone else. She believed Helen's affliction was God's curse.

Meanwhile, Captain Keller, always the hopeful newspaperman, included information about his daughter's condition in the February 10, 1882, issue of *The North Alabamian*:

> In response to many kind inquiries we are happy to announce the probable recovery of our little Girl.

A month later, he laconically reported the results of a trip to a Cincinnati doctor:

> Our friends will sympathize with us on hearing that she is thought to be permanently blind.

In spite of this news, Captain Keller and his wife did not give up trying to find a cure for Helen. For the next six years they spared no expense taking her to every doctor they could find for treatments that ranged from mineral water spas to special "electric" tests. Nothing worked.

It was Helen's good fortune that after she became deaf and blind, she was surrounded by a devoted group of parents, relatives, and servants. She had complete run of the garden and yard and never lacked for a playmate. Often Martha Washington, the daughter of the family's black cook, protected and entertained Helen. Naturally, Helen became almost intolerably spoiled and bossy. But she was bright and touched and explored everything she could. She sat in her mother's lap or clung to her dress as she went about her household duties. "My hands felt every object and observed every motion and in this way I learned to know many things," Helen remembered.

Helen created her own form of "home" sign language. If she wanted bread she imitated the act of cutting bread and spreading butter. If she wanted ice cream, she made the sign of working the freezer crank and then shivered to indicate cold. Her sign for her mother was stroking her cheek. Her sign for her father was to make the shape of spectacles with her fingers against her eyes.

"My earliest distinct recollection of my father is making my way through drifts of newspapers to his side and finding him alone, holding a sheet of paper before his face. I was greatly puzzled to know what he was doing," Helen later wrote. "I imitated this action, even wearing his spectacles, thinking they might help solve the mystery."

Unlike children confined in institutions for the deaf and blind of the time, Helen was not forbidden to use sign language, a language using a complex set of expressive hand and body movements. No teacher spent countless unpleasant hours forcing her to try to speak. Instead, left to her own devices, she learned much from direct experience—touching, smelling, and tasting the world around her.

There were plenty of places to explore: the sheds where the corn was kept, the stable where the horses slept, the yard where the cows were milked. She was always fond of the many animals—her father's horse, his dogs, and an especially tolerant, ancient setter named Belle.

Martha Washington, three years older than tyrannical Helen, knew and obeyed her crude, limited signs. She shared Helen's love of mischief. One hot July day, Helen and Martha became bored cutting paper dolls on the shady veranda steps. After they snipped their shoestrings and shredded

Helen and the cook's daughter spent much time kneading dough balls and quarreling over the cake bowl in this building that housed the kitchen.

honeysuckle leaves into bits, Helen decided to use her scissors to give Martha a new hairdo. Her companion's hair stuck out all over her head in corkscrews. "She objected at first but finally submitted," recalled Helen. Next it was Martha's turn. She had just begun to snip off Helen's long curls when Helen's hysterical mother appeared and stopped the entire hairstyling venture.

When she wasn't playing, Helen helped with chores. At age five, she folded and put away clean clothes when they were brought in from the laundry. She sniffed each piece and knew which garments belonged to her—and she was always right. Helen and Martha spent a lot of time in the kitchen kneading dough balls, making ice cream, grinding coffee, and quarreling over the batter remains in the cake bowl. They fed the hens and turkeys and hunted for eggs in the long grass.

Helen insisted on carrying the eggs home. She told poor Martha with emphatic signs that she might "fall and break them." One time a big gobbler grabbed a tomato out of Helen's hand and ran away. Inspired by the turkey's boldness, Helen decided she'd try a similar trick. She went in the kitchen, stole an entire cake, ran behind the woodpile, and ate the whole thing herself. Soon after she felt very sick to her stomach.

Helen became more frustrated by her inability to communicate as she grew older. She knew she was different. "Sometimes I stood between two persons . . . and touched their lips," she wrote. "I could not understand and was vexed. I moved my lips and gesticulated frantically without result. This made me so angry at times that I kicked and screamed till I was exhausted."

As Helen grew stronger, her tantrums and mischief did more damage. She broke dishes and lamps and grabbed food from people's plates at the dinner table. She nearly set herself on fire trying to dry a wet apron by holding it too close to the flames. Another time she figured out how to use a key and purposefully locked her mother in the pantry for three hours. To her grandmother's horror, she dashed into the parlor wearing only red flannel underwear. Then she pinched and chased the elderly woman, who did not think her granddaughter's antics the least bit amusing.

Some relatives began to call Helen "a wild, destructive animal." One uncle told her mother that she was "mentally defective" and should be put

Before Annie's arrival, Helen remembered coming into the parlor of Ivy Green in her red flannel underwear, pinching Grandma Adams and chasing her from the room.

out of sight in an institution. Loyal Aunt Evaline Keller, Captain Keller's sister, nicknamed Aunt Ev, disagreed. "This child has more sense than all the Kellers," she said, "if there's a way to reach her mind."

The problem was, *how* could anyone reach Helen? No doctor had been helpful. No federal programs existed that could give the Kellers any information or recommend testing or schools. Neither her mother nor her father could bear to send her away to live at the only alternative, the struggling Alabama Institute for the Deaf and Blind, more than one hundred miles away in Talladega. The segregated private boarding school had sixteen white students. Like most blind and deaf children at the time, the students were viewed as "defectives" who might learn to make brooms, weave baskets, or cane chairs, and not much more. Industrial training— not mastering reading or writing—was the institution's main goal.

Alabama Institute for the Deaf and Blind in Talladega in the late 1880s

Alabama had a poor record of taking care of ordinary children, much less those who could not hear or see. The state spent barely one dollar per student per year to support public education. In 1880, more than half of Alabama's children ten years and older could not read or write—an appalling figure considering that nationwide illiteracy had dropped to 17 percent.

In Alabama's backward, underfunded education system, the children the most afflicted were the least served. Little money was available to take care of a community's "unwanted." In fact, since 1830 an Alabama law expressly prevented carnivals from bringing deaf people with them and abandoning them "to local towns for support."

Not only in Alabama but elsewhere throughout the United States, the blind and deaf faced enormous prejudice. Uneducated and thought uneducable, most blind and deaf children were viewed as monstrosities to be feared, pitied, abandoned, shunned, or simply ignored. Some families believed that their deaf or blind children were burdens for them to bear and did not try to "change what God had wrought." Some kept them hidden; others viewed them simply as "good working hands" and refused to provide them with any education.

There were no free state or federally run programs to assist or train the blind and deaf. Children whose families could not afford one of the few privately funded progressive boarding schools like Perkins Institution never learned to read or write. If their families could not provide long-term care, these "defectives," as they were called, ended up in local county asylums for the poor. In *Middletown*, Robert and Helen Lynd's classic sociological study of American life in Muncie, Indiana, the poor asylum of 1890 was described as "the county catch-basin" with living conditions that were "shocking and deplorable." Here the deaf and the blind were housed with "the insane, the feeble-minded, the epileptic . . . the shiftless, the vicious, [the] respectable homeless."

The lucky deaf and blind who had some sort of manual ability might be taken as apprentices to learn simple trades, such as shoe repair. Women who were blind or deaf and had no visible means of support were less

Photographer Lewis Hine recorded this blind beggar and his young guide on the streets of New York City in 1910.

likely to be taught a skill. They never married and, unable to become self-sufficient, were forced to enter asylums for most of their lives.

Like so many marginalized groups of people who seemed different, the blind and deaf were easy to stigmatize. In the late nineteenth century they weren't viewed as people with simply another way of being. They were seen as a calamity—or worse. This tradition of treating the blind and deaf as "flawed" and potentially dangerous went back to early Europe and even further back to ancient Greece and Rome, where blind or deaf babies were abandoned to die along roadsides.

By the 1880s Victorian perceptions about blindness reflected cultural bias. Of all the senses, sight was viewed as the most important. The eyes were seen as "windows to the soul" and could reveal whether an individual was good or bad. Because most information and learning was relayed through sight, vision was viewed as the sense of the intellect. For most Victorians, blindness was perceived as terrifying—something to be dreaded.

To be deaf and dumb (unable to speak) was equated with mental deficiency. English law looked upon a deaf individual as "an idiot . . . incapable of understanding as wanting all those senses which furnish the mind with ideas," wrote Sir William Blackstone (1723–1780) in *Commentaries*. Until the mid-1700s, the deaf in America and elsewhere in Europe were considered incompetent to inherit property, marry, receive an education, or have a job. By the mid-1800s it was still not legal for them to serve on juries, own property, or appear in court. The deaf who used sign language—and thus made their disability visible—were viewed suspiciously by Victorian Americans, who found their method of conversation dangerously "foreign," clannish—even anti-American.

For the desperate parents of six-year-old Helen, the chance of finding any real assistance for her seemed to dwindle to nothing. And then one day by accident Kate Keller picked up a dog-eared copy of a forty-year-old book by English writer Charles Dickens.

For the Kellers and especially for Helen, nothing would ever quite be the same again.

Helen at age seven

3.
The Big Breakthrough

Have you ever been at sea in a dense fog, when it seemed as if a tangible white darkness shut you in, and the great ship, tense and anxious, groped her way toward shore with plummet and sounding-line, and you waited with beating heart for something to happen? I was like that ship before my education began.

—Helen Keller, *The Story of My Life*

KATE KELLER READ *American Notes*, an account of Charles Dickens's 1842 trip to the United States with avid interest. On that journey the English writer described a visit to a remarkable celebrity in Boston. Laura Bridgman, a blind and deaf thirteen-year-old, had miraculously learned to communicate through the efforts of educator Dr. Samuel Gridley Howe at the Perkins Institution for the Blind.

Kate badgered her husband. Couldn't someone do the same for Helen? She used every feminine wile to persuade Captain Keller to make one more trip, one more try. Maybe this time they'd find the help they needed.

Captain Keller was not enthusiastic. Boston was more than a thousand miles away. Worse yet, he discovered that Dr. Howe had died in 1876, more than ten years earlier. Who was to say if his methods had died with him? Laura Bridgman, now nearly fifty-seven, was still living at Perkins—but what help might she be in reaching Helen?

In 1845 blind and deaf sixteen-year-old Laura Bridgman was already a celebrity. Like the other children at Perkins, she wore a ribbon across her closed eyes. When author Charles Dickens met her in 1842, he noticed that her doll wore the same green ribbon "fastened about its mimic eyes."

Perhaps not wishing to disappoint either his desperate wife or his readers, who had been following Helen's saga of trips to doctors in *The North Alabamian*, Captain Keller came up with a compromise. They would go north, but only as far as Baltimore. There they would seek the help of an eminent oculist who was said to specialize in "hopeless cases."

This plan seemed to placate his wife, who enlisted the help of Aunt Ev, who remained Helen's loyal supporter all her life. Amazingly, Helen behaved very well on the long train ride. She amused herself by punching pieces of cardboard with a ticket puncher borrowed from the conductor. She played with a doll Aunt Ev created from a rolled-up towel after insisting her aunt cut two beads from her cape and sew them onto the sightless doll's face for eyes.

However, the trip proved to be another disappointment. The famous Baltimore oculist named Dr. Julian John Chisolm had no good news about Helen's eyes and told Helen's parents the same thing they had already heard countless times. No operation or cure existed. Helen would always be blind and deaf, the specialist emphatically told them.

In spite of the gloomy prediction, he did give them a few words of hope. Why not visit Dr. Alexander Graham Bell, who was a well-known inventor and educator of the deaf? After all, they had come so far, and Dr. Bell was only thirty-five miles away in Washington, D.C.

No record exists describing how Helen's parents felt about meeting

Alexander Graham Bell as he would have appeared when the Keller family met him for the first time in Washington, D.C., in 1886

the famous Bell, who had initially come up with the idea for the telephone in 1876 as a hearing aid for the deaf. Tall and domineering, he had a thick silver beard, sparkling black eyes, and wore his hair brushed back from his forehead. He enjoyed using his loud clear voice to great effect when reciting Shakespeare or singing Scottish songs. Some people called him an overbearing boor. Bell's father described him as "apt to let enthusiasm run away with judgment."

When the Kellers met him, he was a forceful, outspoken man in the prime of his life who was swiftly becoming one of the most influential men in deaf education. He had a deaf mother and his wife was deaf. Bell had very definite ideas about how the deaf ought to behave. His theories represented those of a majority of deaf educators of the late nineteenth century. For Bell, like the others, the deaf should strive to behave as much like the hearing as possible. He did not believe they should use sign language. Instead, he thought that the deaf should train diligently to learn to lipread and eventually acquire oral speech. According to Bell, the deaf should neither intermarry nor congregate in clannish groups.

On a summer evening in 1886, Helen and her family went to Bell's house. This would be the beginning of a lifelong friendship for Helen. She was delighted that Bell let her sit on his knee and "listen" to his pocket watch chime. She used her own "home signs" to ask questions, an indication to Bell that she was bright.

Bell did not approve of promoting such signs, but he understood their rudimentary nature. Although he later wrote that he found Helen's expression "chillingly empty," he was intrigued by her obvious intelligence. Helen seemed good-natured, attractive, and full of energy.

Without making any direct promises, Bell gave Captain Keller the name of yet another educator: Michael Anagnos, the son-in-law of Howe. Anagnos had taken over as director of the Perkins Institution in Boston. In August 1886, Captain Keller wrote a letter to Anagnos to ask if there might be a tutor who could come to Tuscumbia to teach his child.

Anagnos, prompted by the powerful Bell, was thrilled. The school could certainly use the publicity if this little girl from Alabama proved to

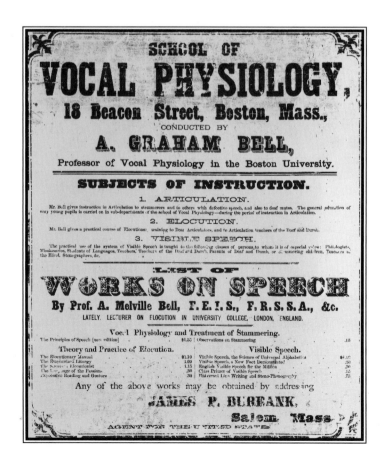

Bell was teaching "visible speech," lip-reading, and speaking to the deaf in Boston in 1880, when Helen was born.

In 1881 fifteen-year-old Annie Sullivan had attended Perkins for almost a year. "My mind was a question mark, my heart a frustration," she wrote.

be "another Laura Bridgman." He wrote back immediately to say that he had a teacher available. Her name was Annie Sullivan.

Annie was gifted, driven, and badly in need of a job since her graduation from Perkins that spring. Captain Keller's offer of twenty-five dollars per month, plus board and washing, must have seemed like a small fortune to twenty-year-old Annie, who was uncertain of her own future. The daughter of an Irish immigrant, she had grown up in poverty. Her father was an abusive alcoholic. Her sickly mother died when Annie was eight years old. Half-blind Annie and her disabled younger brother were abandoned at the state poorhouse in Tewksbury, Massachusetts. She survived six years in the grimy, desolate asylum, which was crowded with 940 men and women—the criminal, diseased, insane, and disabled mixed among the orphaned poor children. Her brother died at age five; "The only thing I had ever loved," she later wrote. Not until Annie was nearly sixty years old would she be able to talk about the abuse, hunger, terror, and loneliness of those years.

Annie convinced the authorities to let her go to school at Perkins. When she entered in 1880, nearly fourteen years old, she owned neither a nightgown nor a hairbrush. She could not read or write and she did not know her own birthday. She spoke with a slight Irish brogue and was filled with intense hate for almost anyone in authority. She knew what it meant to be blind and shuffled out of sight by society. She knew what happened to the deaf who were cast away by their families or circumstance and left to live and die in institutions. In spite of unpromising beginnings, she managed to excel and graduated valedictorian of her class.

Nicknamed "Miss Spitfire" by the Perkins staff, Annie was fiery, tough, and ambitious. She had only six months to prepare to teach Helen. "I seized upon the first opportunity that offered itself, although I did not suspect, nor did [Anagnos] that I had any special fitness for the work," she wrote.

Annie had no training, no special skills, and no experience. No seasoned instructor was available to her to help her get ready to go to Alabama. She took a crash course in finger spelling, the method of communication that Laura Bridgman had learned as a child. Although her own sight was poor and her inflamed eyes were often weepy and red, she read everything Howe had written about Laura Bridgman. She frequently visited the frail Bridgman, to whom she finger-spelled the latest gossip.

As the day for Annie's departure drew closer, the students at Perkins threw themselves into preparation. The blind girls in the grade school made Helen a special doll. Anagnos presented Annie with a garnet ring and a paid train ticket to Tuscumbia. Still, she felt unprepared and unsuitably dressed in her frumpy dark blue dress and hideous black satin bonnet. The only stylish item of clothing she could afford was a new pair of high-buttoned shoes that were too small.

The two-day train trip was the farthest she'd ever traveled in her life. Because of her sore eyes, severely inflamed from a recent operation, she had to wear dark glasses. Annie had contracted trachoma when she was about five years old. If untreated, this disease eventually causes blindness. She spent so much time crying on the train that the conductor assumed she was on her way to a funeral. To make matters worse, her stylish shoes blistered her feet and she was forced to shuffle about instead in her old felt slippers.

On March 3, she finally arrived exhausted and dust-covered on the little platform in Tuscumbia. She was met by Kate Keller and her stepson, James, who had driven a carriage to the station to meet every train for the past two days. Due to a miscommunication, no one was sure when Annie would arrive.

The carriage ambled down Tuscumbia's broad main street lined with magnolias toward the Keller home. The first thing that surprised Annie was the quietness of the countryside—so different from bustling Boston or the crowded state poorhouse in Tewksbury. The second surprise was Mrs. Keller's youthfulness. Kate Keller was only ten years older than Annie.

More than anything, Annie wanted to meet her new pupil. "I tried with all my might to control the eagerness that made me tremble so that I could hardly walk," Annie wrote three days after her arrival in a letter to a friend at Perkins. Finally, she spotted Helen waiting in the porch doorway at Ivy Green. She had expected to see a pale, delicate child. "But there's nothing pale or delicate about Helen," Annie admitted. "She is strong, and ruddy, and as unrestrained in her movements as a young colt."

Annie was relieved that Helen was not deformed, something that she had a personal aversion to all her life. She was also glad that Helen displayed none of the nervous tics and mannerisms—swaying side to side, moving her hands in front of her face—that many blind children developed. "Her body," Annie noted, "is well formed and vigorous. . . . She has a fine head and it is set on her shoulders just right." Helen's face looked intelligent, but her mouth, though "large and finely shaped," rarely broke into a smile.

Annie had just shaken hands with Captain Keller in greeting and took a few steps up to the porch to meet Helen, when the little girl rushed at her "with such a force that she would have thrown me backward if Captain Keller had not been behind me."

The first thing Helen did was to feel Annie's face and dress and bag. She had had enough experience with visitors and their luggage to know that they often brought along sweets as presents for her. She searched Annie's luggage. She felt for a keyhole and made a sign of turning a key and pointing to the bag. After a tussle between Helen and her embarrassed mother over the suitcase, Annie distracted Helen with her watch and convinced her to follow her upstairs to help her unpack. Helen tried on Annie's bonnet, cocking her head from side to side at the mirror just as her mother probably did before going out.

As soon as Annie unpacked her trunk, she began her first lesson with Helen, who found the doll and held it tight. Annie spelled "D-O-L-L" into Helen's hand. She placed Helen's hand so that she could feel her pointing to the doll and nodding her head, signs that meant that the doll was a gift.

Helen looked puzzled by this stranger's behavior. She felt Annie's hand and she repeated the letters again for her. "She imitated them very well and pointed to the doll," Annie remembered. Then she took the doll away from Helen, planning to give it back to her after she spelled "doll" correctly. Unfortunately, Helen thought she meant to take the doll away and had a tantrum.

Annie kept the doll and ran downstairs to find a piece of cake, which she hoped to use as a bribe. She showed Helen the cake and spelled "C-A-K-E" into her hand. Helen made the letters rapidly. "I gave her the cake, which she ate in a great hurry, thinking I suppose that I might take it from her."

The first lesson ended unsuccessfully. Helen had no idea that the strange finger shapes this stranger persisted in making into her hand had anything to do with the objects she was being shown.

The next several days proved to be a series of "battle royals" between Annie and her new charge, who preferred to wander about the table during meals and plunge her hands into everyone's plates. No one, least of all her doting father, had ever bothered to discipline Helen. Naturally, the family looked on in alarm when Annie tried to force Helen to learn table manners. When Annie's attempts met with failure, she ordered everyone except Helen to leave the room. Annie locked the dining room door.

Helen kicked and screamed on the floor. She tried to pull Annie's chair out from under her as she continued trying to eat. She hurled spoons. She pinched. She shoved. Annie forced Helen to pick up the spoon and eat with it. She forced her to fold her napkin. This went on for several hours.

Captain Keller and his family wondered if they had made a terrible mistake hiring this Yankee teacher.

When the row ended, Helen was finally let out into the warm sunshine. In minutes, she was back to her bratty ways, bossing her poor beleaguered father, mother, and playmates. Annie went upstairs to her room for a good cry.

A week after her arrival, Annie finally managed to convince Kate Keller that she had to have Helen by herself for any progress to be made. Captain Keller allowed her to keep Helen with her alone at the Little House, away from the intrusions of the rest of her family. Helen brought along her favorite doll, Nancy—besmeared with mud pies and frazzled and worn with use.

Captain Keller drove Helen in the wagon in a roundabout route to the Little House, which had been reorganized so that Helen did not recognize where she was. A young servant boy took care of the fireplace. The cook brought food from the kitchen.

At first Helen was homesick and angry and refused to go to sleep in the same bed with Annie. Eventually, she did go to sleep after a two-hour fight. "Fortunately for us both, I am a little stronger, and quite as obstinate when I set out," Annie wrote. Their days were spent in the garden.

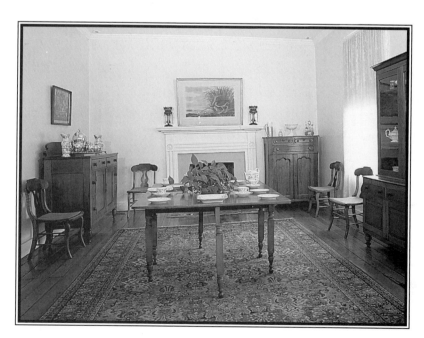

The dining room of Ivy Green became the site of "a test of wills" between Helen and Annie, who was determined to teach her new pupil manners.

The Little House, where Helen lived alone with Annie during the spring of 1887

Sullivan taught her new words, still aware, however, that Helen did not make any real connection between the wiggling finger movements and the objects themselves.

When her old dog, Belle, was brought to the Little House, Helen was overjoyed. She put her arms around her old companion's neck and squeezed her, then sat down beside her and began to manipulate her paws to try to teach the dog how to finger-spell "doll."

After a week in isolation, Helen's family insisted she be brought home. Immediately, conflicts erupted. Who was in charge of Helen—her parents or Annie? Stubbornly, Annie held her ground. For the next two weeks, she spelled into Helen's hand everything they did all day long, even though Helen still did not really understand what the finger spelling meant.

The big breakthrough came on a warm spring morning, April 3, 1887, a month after Annie's arrival. Whenever Helen wanted to know the name for something, she would pat Annie's hand and point to the object. It was a kind of game for a bright child with a very good memory who had learned how to finger-spell more than twenty words—everything from "eye" to "walk."

But Helen still had trouble understanding the difference between "milk" and "mug" and what it meant to "drink" something. That morning she had asked Annie how to finger-spell "water." Annie had shown her the spelling and did not think much more about it until after breakfast, when she decided perhaps there might be another way to help Helen understand.

"We went out to the pump-house," Annie wrote, "and I made Helen hold her mug under the spout while I pumped." While cold water gurgled and gushed and splashed into the mug, Annie finger-spelled "W-A-T-E-R" into Helen's free hand. "The word coming so close upon the sensation of cold water rushing over her hand seemed to startle her. She dropped the mug and stood as one transfixed. A new light came into her face. She spelled 'water' several times."

The realization was electrifying. Helen had recalled from before her illness, from deep in her earliest childhood, one of the very first words she ever spoke: "Wa-wa." *W-a-t-e-r.* In one split second, everything changed for Helen. She had discovered language.

"Suddenly, I felt a misty consciousness as of something forgotten—a thrill of returning thought," remembered Helen. "I knew that 'w-a-t-e-r' meant the wonderful cool something that was flowing over my hand."

The first thing she did was drop to her knees and put her hands on the ground and ask for its name. She asked for the name of the pump, the name for the trellis. And suddenly, in one swift movement, she turned around and pointed to Annie. What was her name? "T-E-A-C-H-E-R," Annie spelled into her hand. This was the name that Helen would call her the rest of her life.

Helen discovered the meaning of "W-A-T-E-R" spelled into her hand by her teacher at this pump near the cookhouse. In 1922 the pump was protected by a simple roofed structure and enclosed with a fence.

Helen in 1888 had learned to read using Braille. With her right hand she quickly formed the letters using the manual alphabet.

4.

So Much to Ask About

Indeed, everything that could hum, or buzz or sing, or
bloom, had a part in my education.
——Helen Keller, *The Story of My Life*

FROM THE MOMENT Helen woke up in the morning until the time she
went to bed, she finger-spelled back and forth with Annie. To understand
a new word, Helen placed her hand lightly on one of Annie's hands and
felt her finger positions change as she spelled individual letters. Annie was
fast and flexible and could finger-spell almost as rapidly as an expert on a
manual typewriter. Constant practice made Helen so adept at interpreting
what Annie was spelling that she did not need to feel each letter in a familiar word, but could simply guess what the word was by picking up the
meaning of the first few letters. Annie treated Helen exactly like a hearing
child acquiring language. She finger-spelled complete sentences into her
hand and filled out the meaning with gestures and descriptive signs. With
each passing hour of each passing day, Helen eagerly demanded to know
the names of everything.

Annie and Helen spent their days outdoors. "All my early lessons have
in them the breath of the woods——the fine, resinous odor of pine needles,
blended with the perfume of wild grapes," Helen later wrote. Often they
took a dirt road that wound among trees and open meadow to Keller's
Landing, a rotted abandoned wharf along the rushing Tennessee River.

Original bridges spanning the Tennessee River near Tuscumbia were destroyed during the Civil War. The structures were gradually rebuilt for railroad travel during the next thirty years.

Helen and her teacher dug dams using pebbles and made islands of sand on the riverbank to study geography. They used shells and fossils to investigate botany and wriggling, growing tadpoles to explore biology.

Helen's family became worried when it seemed that their daughter had become too zealous in her pursuit of knowledge. They fretted when she would rather finger-spell than eat. Anxious that she might be sick, her father called the doctor. He announced that Helen was "thinking too much." But when Annie tried to give finger spelling a rest, Helen carried on lively conversation with herself. "Even when she sleeps," Annie wrote, "her fingers are spelling the confused and rambling dream-thoughts."

Annie and her teaching had a remarkable effect on Helen. At the same time, Helen changed her teacher. Annie later said that Helen made her more conscious of sensations that she never paid much attention to before—everything from the scent of ripe wild strawberries to the shady smell under a rotting log. "Indeed," she confessed, "I feel as if I had never seen anything until now, Helen finds so much to ask about along the way."

In early June, when the heat became nearly unbearable, Annie discovered that Helen had been observing her very carefully as she wrote with a Braille slate, poking raised dots in paper with a special stylus or pen. Helen, who regularly accompanied Annie on trips to the post office, knew that Annie wrote letters to "little blind girls."

One day Helen appeared with a piece of paper punched with Braille dots. She demanded that Annie put it in an envelope and take it to the post office. Annie wondered to whom the letter was addressed.

"Frank," Helen replied, indicating her uncle.

What did the letter say?

"Much words," Helen explained proudly. "Puppy motherdog—five. Baby—cry. Hot. Helen walk—no. Sunfire—bad. Frank—come. Helen—kiss Frank. Strawberries—very good."

Clearly, Helen was ready to learn to read. Annie obliged, teaching her how a certain pattern of raised dots meant the same as one letter in the finger-spelled alphabet. Helen ran her finger over the dots and put words together. Her memory was so good, she was soon able to read very easy sentences in Braille. Reading became a passion she would have all her life. "In a word, literature is my Utopia," she later wrote. "Here I am not disenfranchised. No barrier of the senses shuts me out."

Helen could not learn fast enough. Her word mastery was amazing, even a little terrifying to her teacher, who struggled to stay ahead of her voracious pupil and her endless questions: *Who puts chickens in eggs? Why is Viney black? Where did Leila get a new baby? What color is think?*

By September 1887, Helen's vocabulary had increased to six hundred words. She did not always use words correctly. Annie sometimes described her sentences as "Chinese puzzles" that had to be interpreted. Words were powerful to Helen. They had smell, taste, even a certain feel. "Language," one close friend later said, "was her way to outward things."

While Helen wrote in Braille, she also practiced writing using a pencil and paper fitted over a grooved writing board to help her keep a straight line. She wrote in a neat square hand, although she could not see what she wrote. In September she received her first letter addressed to her from an uncle. It was a handwritten invitation to visit him in Hot Springs. Annie read the letter to Helen using finger spelling. Helen asked many questions before finding her mother and finger-spelling everything Annie had told her word for word.

Then she tried to force baby Mildred and the old setter Belle to sit through another finger-spelling performance. Mildred wasn't interested. Belle had other things on her mind. But Helen persisted even when Mildred tried to nibble the letter and the dog attempted to escape. Helen grabbed the dog by her neck and made her sit down. Meanwhile, Mildred had vanished. So had the letter.

Helen stood perfectly still, trying to sense the patter of her baby sister's feet on the floor. She made a high-pitched "baby" call she used sometimes to get Mildred's attention. When she found Mildred, she was chewing happily on the letter. Helen grabbed it and smacked her sister on the hand.

At this point, her mother and Annie rescued screaming Mildred. "What did you do to baby?" Annie demanded.

"Wrong girl did eat letter. Helen did slap very wrong girl," Helen replied.

Annie tried to explain to Helen that her sister was too young to know what she was doing. Helen refused to accept this excuse. "I did tell baby no, no, no many times."

"Mildred doesn't understand your fingers, and you must be gentle with her."

Helen ran upstairs. She returned with a carefully folded piece of paper

The master bedroom at Ivy Green belonged to Helen's parents. On the bed is a quilt sewn by Helen's beloved Aunt Ev.

Annie Sullivan in 1887, the year she arrived in Tuscumbia

poked with many Braille dots. "Baby not think. Helen will give baby pretty letter." She handed the paper to Mildred. "Baby can eat all words."

As Helen's reading ability improved, she became frustrated when she could find few Braille books to read on her own. Annie did the best she could to finger-spell stories that appealed to her. But even Annie had her limits. Once when she was too exhausted to read more from the novel *Little Lord Fauntleroy*, Helen recalled feeling for the first time "a keen sense of my deprivations. I took the book in my hands and tried to feel the printed letters with an intensity of longing that I can never forget."

Helen often tried to read at night when she was supposed to be sleeping. Once when caught in the act, Helen claimed that she'd taken the book to bed with her because it was fearful. "Book cry," she told Annie.

Annie, never easily tricked, told her that the book wasn't weeping or afraid and must sleep in the bookcase.

Helen tried to appear cowed. She looked "very roguish," Annie said, "and apparently understood that I saw through her ruse."

After only two months in Tuscumbia, Annie had made such incredible progress with her pupil that she began to view her success in a whole new way. "I shall succeed beyond my wildest dreams," she confided to a friend. She was convinced that Helen's education would even surpass in interest and wonder Dr. Howe's achievement with Laura Bridgman. "She is no ordinary child and people's interest in her education will be no ordinary interest."

Annie was proud and had a youthful and somewhat immature view of her own prospects for fame and that of her student. Although Annie stated deceptively in a letter to a friend, "My beautiful Helen shall not be transformed into a prodigy if I can help it," her actions were quite contradictory. Transforming Helen into a well-publicized prodigy was exactly what she wanted.

There was a dramatic difference between Christmas of 1887 and the previous holiday, when Helen had still been "untamed." Annie was pleased to report that her employers were suitably grateful on Christmas morning. Even Captain Keller, whose relationship with the Yankee teacher was often rather prickly, seemed so overcome with emotion he could not say a word.

In spite of her success, Annie was becoming restless. She found the small-town culture of Tuscumbia boring. "Nothing happens day after day, and life is as monotonous as the song of the whippoorwill," she complained. Her hair-trigger temper and extreme opinions soon got her into arguments. After one disagreement with Captain Keller about the Civil War, she stomped upstairs, packed her bags, and prepared to leave. Only clever and persistent pleading by Helen's mother persuaded her to stay.

Helen was probably aware of the periodic battles in the household. She had an uncanny ability to perceive the state of mind of those around her. Her very survival depended on her ability to read body movements—moments when people near her became tense or acted abruptly or impatiently.

What Helen might not have sensed was how possessive her teacher was becoming of her. Annie had become Helen's "substitute mother" and had assumed all care of her twenty-four hours a day. Annie tried to be careful not to alienate Kate Keller, who could finger-spell. But she jealously controlled who was allowed to speak directly to Helen. She resented when Captain Keller or anyone else taught Helen what she considered "unauthorized" words.

"Helen's dependence on me for almost everything makes me strong and glad," she confided to a friend in a letter on New Year's Day. Unlike Annie's ailing mother or little brother, Helen was someone she was certain would not abandon her. "I have found a real friend—one who will never get away from me, or try to, or want to."

Helen and Annie became inseparable. "I spelled into her hand a description of what was taking place around us," Annie later wrote. "What I saw; what others were doing; anything, everything." She spoke to Helen in complete finger-spelled sentences and insisted Helen do the same.

Annie's innovative teaching method was based on her own observations about how hearing and seeing children learned through direct, constant contact. Her goal was not simply to give Helen a vocabulary. She wanted to teach Helen how to think, question, and observe.

In the beginning there was no rigid plan. Helen's curiosity and interest launched every lesson. A trip to the circus became an opportunity to find out about faraway countries and sit on a camel's back. When Helen became fascinated by insects, Annie caught a bug and allowed her to investigate its delicate wings and antennae before letting it go free. On their walks in the garden, fields, or along the water's edge, Annie encouraged Helen to describe in detail everything familiar—and unfamiliar. "She learned to feel," Annie said, "as if every little blade of grass had a history."

When Helen posed with Jumbo in 1887 she was already world-famous.

5.

No Ordinary Child

Mr. Drew says little girls in China cannot talk on their
fingers but I think when I go to China I will teach them.
—Helen's letter to her mother from Boston,
September 24, 1888

$\mathcal{H}$ELEN KELLER'S DISCOVERY by the American media in 1888 came at a
perfect moment.

Americans during the last part of the nineteenth century had experienced swift, dizzying changes—everything from the appearance of
electricity to the disappearance of the frontier. Transportation and communication boomed. Americans had more and faster trains, electric trol-
leys, and steamships than ever before. They could communicate across the
continent with telegraphs and, later, with telephones. Newspapers and
magazines were being mass-produced and distributed from coast to coast.
In New Jersey, a brilliant, irritable man named Thomas Edison was busy
perfecting incandescent light, which he invented in 1879, and the phono-
graph, which he developed in 1877. By 1896 he presented the first com-
mercial showing of a projected moving picture in New York City.

Railroad tracks crisscrossed the continent. The 35,000 miles of track in
1865 had multiplied nearly five times to 193,000 miles by 1900. There
were more trains in the United States moving more goods than anywhere
else in the world. With what one historian called a "fierce adolescent joy,"
American industry dug up vast resources of minerals, leveled seemingly
endless forests, and piped out oil and gas to create so many new products

that by the turn of the century the United States had become the leading manufacturer in the world.

It was a frenzied time. New technology and new, disturbing scientific theories contributed to a vague sense of general uneasiness. Since the mid-nineteenth century, American debate had raged over the ideas of English scientist Charles Darwin. His books, *The Origin of the Species* and *The Descent of Man*, seemed to imply that man was not created directly by God but had evolved over time from apes through "natural selection." Horrified individuals claimed that Darwin challenged the idea of a God-centered universe. Darwin enthusiasts believed that on the eve of the twentieth century, scientists, philosophers, and others should be given free reign to explore a whole new range of possibilities about how life on Earth started.

Many Americans were expressing a growing sense of confusion and disillusionment about the future. "Never was there, perhaps, more hollowness at heart than at present," poet and journalist Walt Whitman wrote in *Democratic Vistas* in 1871. For Whitman, people in cities had become "hurrying, feverish electric crowds." Where were they going? What were they doing?

Other Americans, who called themselves Nativists, declared their own deep-seated fears. Who were all these thousands of non-English-speaking people who poured onto America's shores? The year 1882 peaked with nearly 789,000 immigrants to America, mostly from northern and western Europe, but by 1902 that number had leaped to 1,285,000. The new immigrants came from southern and eastern Europe, places like Italy and Bulgaria and Russia. Often described as a "darker race," these new immigrants did not speak English or worship in Protestant churches. There was something vaguely threatening and disturbing about these new faces to Nativist Americans, who had been in the country long enough to worry that their jobs might be taken away from them by newcomers.

In spite of feverish technological, scientific, and social change, most people in the United States remained deeply religious. They were fascinated with the idea of "striving," a popular term that referred to the idea of combining religious feeling and educational earnestness. A growing network of self-improvement enterprises—fairs, museums, libraries, college examination courses, women's clubs, night schools, and professional societies—sprang up across the country.

No person better represented this striving ideal than the amazing, winsome Helen Keller, who seemed to have beaten all odds by learning to communicate. To imagine someone awakened by language proved to many striving Americans that, contrary to Darwin, humans must have souls touched by a divine spark after all.

Helen's story—elaborate, dramatic, and larger than life—was told in flowery, excessive language that was the fashion of the day. "History presents no case like hers," claimed the account from Perkins Institution published in 1888. "As if impelled by a resistless instinctive force she snatched the key of the treasury of the English language from the fingers of her teacher, unlocked its doors with vehemence, and began to feast on its contents with inexpressible delight. . . . [H]er mental faculties emerged full-armed from their living tomb as Pallas Athene from the head of Zeus."

In newspapers across America Helen Keller was viewed as a phenomenon. She seemed to represent something pure and precious and good that was so clearly missing from the ordinary hustle and bustle of the lives of most Americans. Attractively dressed in white frocks with her chestnut hair curled, photogenic Helen appeared in carefully posed pictures that showed her in profile so that her protruding left eye was not noticeable.

Weekly developments in her education were exaggerated and transmitted around the world. Newspaper accounts told how she learned to play the piano and read people's minds. In Europe everyone from parlor maids to royalty followed Helen's story with avid interest. In America she entranced philosophers, clergymen, and scientists. She inspired poets.

She appealed to everyone—no matter what their outlook. Was there ever anyone so untouched? She had no vanity because, according to one wistful European noblewoman, she had never seen her own face in a mirror.

Unaware of the public's growing interest in her life, Helen responded to letters from Anagnos and others with charming, open enthusiasm. In 1888, Helen had been influenced enough by Annie's glowing reports about

Boston to write directly to Anagnos and suggest that she'd like to visit the "little blind girls." Anagnos, who was having trouble raising money for his new kindergarten, was delighted to have Helen tour Perkins and stay as long as she liked. The trip—Helen's first big outing—promised to be a major media event. It was also Annie's big chance to escape Alabama.

Anagnos and Helen wrote letters back and forth. Little did Helen or her family know that her correspondence was being published almost as soon as it arrived in Boston.

Soon letters from other famous people began to come to the house addressed to Helen. Dr. Edward Everett Hale, a social reformer who was a distant cousin on her mother's side, wrote a long article about Helen in his magazine. Dr. Alexander Graham Bell expressed delight in his letters that Helen was coming to the East Coast to visit. He leaked all her correspondence to him plus a photo of her taken in 1888 to *Science Monthly*—much to her family's chagrin. Everyone seemed eager to cash in on the Helen Keller phenomenon.

Reporters began to show up at the house to ask for interviews. Captain Keller sent the newspapermen away. However, that spring he was not adverse to showing off his daughter before a group of physicians in Cincinnati or the entire congregation at church. The churchgoers laughed

Eight-year-old Helen wrote this letter in pencil to Cousin George.

at her antics when she loudly sniffed the wine during Communion, then tried to kiss everyone. "Wherever she went she was the center of interest," Annie grumbled.

Tension built as Helen, her mother, and Annie prepared for their mid-May trip to Boston. On the way they stopped in Memphis to visit relatives. Admirers invited Helen to countless outings, dinners, and teas. "Helen was petted and caressed enough to spoil an angel," Annie wrote, "but I do not think it possible to spoil her; she is too unconscious of herself and too loving."

Another side trip was a visit to Washington, D.C., where, on the insistence of Captain Keller, Helen met President Cleveland at the White House. It should have been a triumphant moment for the daughter of an avowed Democrat who needed all the political pull he had to keep his new job as county sheriff. "I was a demonstrative, affectionate child," Helen later admitted, "and my first thought was to kiss the President. Not understanding my intentions, or perhaps understanding them only too well, he pushed me away. I am ashamed to confess that I was never able to see much good in Cleveland's administration after that."

A more successful visit was to the home of Bell, who seemed impressed by Helen's progress and spoke to her very quickly using finger spelling about lions, tigers, and elephants. Helen was thrilled when he promised to send her a toy elephant. Annie was not so delighted, however, when Bell also showed Helen a special glove with letters on each part of the fingers. This "talking glove" was designed to allow anyone to communicate easily with someone who was blind and deaf. It would have been especially helpful to Captain Keller, who did not know finger spelling very well.

However, moody, possessive Annie discouraged any such use of the glove. She did not want "irresponsible and unreasoning persons to have easy access to my darling's pure and loving heart. I am determined to keep my beautiful treasure unspotted from the world."

Helen's entrance into Boston high society and "learned circles" was a triumph. Annie felt left out and angry when she thought people treated her only as Helen's servant. Perhaps to boost her own self-image, she went to a shop with Helen in tow and spent her entire salary on a handsome fur-lined velvet cape. It was clearly not clothing for someone trapped in

In 1892 Helen posed at Perkins with another blind-deaf student, Edith Thomas. This photo is unusual because it shows Helen's malformed left eye.

the overheated confines of Tuscumbia. This rash and spontaneous purchase would be characteristic of her spending habits the rest of her life.

At Perkins Institution Helen made many new friends and enjoyed knitting, working with clay, and doing beadwork. She was the star attraction at the commencement exercises, where she held a standing-room-only crowd enthralled while she finger-spelled a poem and gracefully skipped back to her seat.

One of the last official visits Helen and Annie made before leaving Perkins for a summer on the seashore at Cape Cod was a visit to another Perkins resident, Laura Bridgman, who was now nearly fifty-nine years old (she would live only one more year). Thin and bespectacled with darkened wire-rim glasses, she sat beside the window crocheting lace in her spotless, well-ordered room. For more than four decades she had been the Perkins celebrity and center of attention. She left the institution twice and had to return because she became withdrawn, sickly, and confused.

Outside the walls of Perkins, the world had changed since Bridgman was a famous little girl. She was once the darling of writers like Dickens and Thomas Carlyle, who celebrated mute women as "speechless heroines" and "redemptive angels" in their novels. Cranky and withdrawn, Bridgman, with her hair pulled back in a severe bun, seemed distant, old-fashioned, and unappealing—perhaps even a little frightening. Although she made noises, some very "unladylike," according to the Perkins staff, Bridgman had never been taught to speak aloud.

As soon as Annie and Helen approached, Bridgman recognized Annie's hand and seemed glad to see her. Bridgman gave Helen a perfunctory kiss. When rambunctious Helen tried to inspect her lacework, she pulled it out of her reach. "I'm afraid your hands are not clean," she primly told Helen.

What Helen really wanted to do was feel Bridgman's face, "but she shrank away like a mimosa blossom from my peering fingers," Helen remembered. "My strong, impulsive movements disturbed her greatly."

"You have not taught her to be very gentle," Bridgman complained to Annie. Then she turned to Helen and emphasized her disapproval by finger spelling emphatically, "You must not be forward when calling on a lady."

When Helen, unable to think of what to do to meet with the haughty woman's approval, decided to sit on the floor, Bridgman yanked her up and reminded her not to dirty her dress. The meeting ended nearly as badly as it had begun. As Helen left, she tried to kiss Bridgman good-bye but instead trampled her toes.

Helen was undoubtedly glad to escape. "To me," she later confessed, "she seemed like a statue I had once felt in a garden; she was so motionless, and her hands were so cool, like flowers that have grown in shady places."

Eight-year-old Helen could not have known that it was Bridgman— so strange and distant—who had paved the way for her own path to fame.

Laura Bridgman in 1885 demonstrated how she could thread a needle with her tongue. She created beautiful lacework and crocheting, which were sold to visitors with her autograph.

Five-year-old Tommy Stringer from Pittsburgh (bottom right) was rescued from the alms house by Helen (top left) who raised money to bring him to Perkins. Also pictured in 1891 are blind-deaf students Edith Thomas (top right) and Elizabeth Robbins (bottom left).

6.

An Unexpected Shift in the Wind

Beneath all the gaiety . . . the oppressive sense of coming ill that made my heart heavy.

—Helen Keller, *The Story of My Life*

ON AND OFF DURING THE SCHOOL YEARS from 1888 until 1892, Helen was an unofficial student at Perkins. She attended tuition-free classes in basketry, clay modeling, and music. She had free run of the school's impressive library of Braille books, gymnasium, and collection of stuffed birds and animals. During this time she studied French and other foreign languages with surprising success. In 1890 she insisted on being taught to speak in outside private lessons given to her by Sarah Fuller, principal of the Horace Mann School for the Deaf. Helen placed her hand on her teacher's throat and lips and tried to imitate the shape of her mouth and tongue. She struggled to copy the right volume of air and push this through her own lips in order to make sounds she couldn't hear.

The months she spent at Perkins with Annie were among Helen's first extended trips away from Tuscumbia and her family. In surviving letters to her mother and Aunt Ev, Helen reports her many activities and new friends but does not mention missing familiar people and places. A hint of her homesickness is revealed, however, in a letter she wrote in 1889 to her philanthropist friend, William Wade. She thanked him for sending her a mastiff puppy named Lioness as a gift, then added, "I hope [the puppy] is not lonely and unhappy. I think puppies can feel very home-sick, as well as little girls."

When Helen was about to turn eleven in 1891, life seemed grand and full of promise. She had many new friends. Her impressive vocabulary now included smatterings of Greek, Latin, and French. In her spare time, she read and corresponded with the rich and famous, including writer Dr. Oliver Wendell Holmes and poet John Greenleaf Whittier. All her letters were scrupulously screened and double-checked by Annie, who made Helen rewrite the whole thing if she found one misspelled word.

When at home in Tuscumbia, Helen was surrounded by a proud, loving family, which included a sister, now six, and a brand-new baby brother, Phillips. She had plenty of pets, including Lioness, the now huge, full-grown mastiff, her own pony named Black Beauty, and a "fat and lazy" donkey called Neddy, all given to her by admirers. She was still young enough to play with her numerous dolls. She wore her hair long, her dress several inches above her shoes. She could still romp and no one found it unladylike or unacceptable.

And yet, like an unexpected, barely perceptible shift in the wind, everything was beginning to change.

The first hint had come three years earlier. In 1888 Captain Keller lost his politically appointed job as United States marshal for northern Alabama. One night at dinner after the disastrous election, Helen cheerfully suggested that they all move to Boston and live in a big house. When her weary father tried to explain that such a move would be very costly, she replied, "You must work very hard and get a great deal of money."

Economic advice from his perky daughter was probably not appreciated by Captain Keller, who was going deeper and deeper into debt. By 1891, he had not paid Annie's salary in almost three years.

Other unsettling hints of change had appeared as early as the summer of 1889, when Helen clearly began to outstrip her teacher's abilities. She had not learned much math because Annie despised the subject. Annie did not know any foreign languages. She subscribed to no religious faith and was uncomfortable answering Helen's constant questions about heaven and hell and death. There were many things about life that perplexed inexperienced twenty-three-year-old Annie. But she refused to let Helen go. She did not want her to receive regular, extended classroom training from other educators.

Years later, when Helen was grown, she recognized that her teacher needed a teacher. "In a sense [we] were growing up together," wrote Helen. "It was not simply knowledge she wanted, but choice English for herself and [me] . . . and a thousand little graces and amenities which betoken true culture and refinement."

To make up for her own shortcomings, Annie pushed herself and her pupil relent-

Perkins director Anagnos reported in 1891 that poised, eleven-year-old Helen "has grown amazingly fast in body and mind alike."

lessly until her own eyesight worsened and she had to go away to Boston for an operation. For almost three months during the summer of 1889 she and Helen were apart—the first time they were separated in two years. Helen must have felt neglected as her exhausted mother struggled to care for Mildred and Phillips while keeping the house running on an ever-shrinking budget. On August 7 Helen wrote a pleading letter to her teacher:

I read in my books every day. I love them very very much. I do want you to come to me soon. I miss you very very much.

I cannot know about many things when my dear teacher is not here. I send you 5,000 kisses, and more love than I can tell.

As Helen pointed out in her letter, what she was learning came almost entirely from her teacher and from books, which concentrated on descriptions of sights and sounds. Unlike a hearing or sighted child, Helen had few opportunities to understand the world directly by listening to conversations between different people or making her own observations with her own eyes.

Although language had freed Helen, it had in some ways also imprisoned her. Like a lonely space explorer on a deep space probe, she was being fed constant long-distance transmissions that she could not explore herself using her own senses of smell, touch, and taste. She could not verify what she was learning through her own experience.

None of these limitations bothered Helen at this point. And why should they? Every day she delighted in the free-fall discovery of new ideas. Eagerly, she experienced the music of poetry and the magic of fairy tales. With clearly defined heroes and evildoers, fairy tales appealed to the way Helen viewed the world—good versus bad.

Her amazing memory stored these growing layers of abstract concepts and phrases verbatim. She wrote far beyond her age level. Her work dazzled everyone.

In September, when Annie returned from Boston, it was clear that Helen needed to start school. She went to Perkins with Annie in the fall of 1889 to begin classes. For the next several years Helen thrived, while restless Annie soon found herself making enemies among the other Perkins teachers by openly criticizing their methods and abilities and currying favor with its director, Michael Anagnos.

Meanwhile, Anagnos made ample use of the glowing details about Helen's progress in annual reports for Perkins, which were largely devoted to her accomplishments. The publicity generated by these reports was immediately embellished in newspapers and magazines throughout the country and around the world. These articles provided spectacular promotion for the school. It seemed as if anything Helen said or did or wrote made great copy. Everyone everywhere wanted to read about the amazing Helen Keller, "child of the spotless brow."

One day at dinner in early fall 1891, while visiting her family in Tuscumbia, Helen entertained her parents and relatives with a fairy story she wrote called "Autumn Leaves." It had been inspired, she said, by the change of seasons. Her parents declared her a marvel. To think that only three years earlier their little daughter could barely sit at the table and eat! Now she was writing impressive stories about King Frost who lived in a beautiful palace "far to the north, in the land of perpetual snow."

Upon Helen's generous suggestion, Annie quickly sent off the story (with the title changed now to "The Frost King") to Anagnos as a special birthday gift. He declared the story "a precious gift" and promised to print it in the next Perkins annual report. "If there be a pupil in any of the private or public grammar schools of New England who can write an original story like this, without assistance from anyone," he bragged, "he or she certainly is a rare phenomenon."

Anagnos's words would soon come back to haunt him.

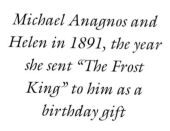

Michael Anagnos and Helen in 1891, the year she sent "The Frost King" to him as a birthday gift

So certain that this story would be a hit, he rushed it for publication to *The Mentor*, the Perkins alumni association journal. Almost immediately the story was printed by *The Goodson Gazette*, a weekly published by the Virginia Institution for the Education of the Deaf and Dumb and the Blind, with a note stating: "We believe it to be without parallel in the history of literature."

Then the bomb dropped.

A reader wrote to the *Gazette* to say that the story by the renowned Helen Keller was copied almost word for word from Margaret T. Canby's children's book, *Birdie and his Fairy Friends*, published in 1874. The editor of the *Gazette* quickly printed this apology:

> The *Goodson Gazette* does not blame little Helen Keller for the attempt as fraud, far from it. She is not to blame. She has merely done what she was told to do. The blame for the fraud rests not upon her, but upon whoever knowingly attempted to palm off "The Frost King" as her composition and there the blame will lie.

To humiliated Anagnos, this was a terrible blow. For years he had promoted Helen Keller as a miracle and Annie Sullivan as the Perkins-inspired miracle worker. What if Helen were a sham? What if her teacher were a fraud? Everything he stood for would be under question.

Anagnos questioned Helen and her family. He drilled Annie, who reacted in the way she always did when she was threatened. She became furious and defensive. She found others to blame. Was it her fault that Mrs. Sophia C. Hopkins had probably read the Canby story to Helen back in 1888 while on a visit to her home in Brewster, Massachusetts?

It's hard to imagine how distressed Helen must have felt when she learned of the uproar. Plagiarism, the willful copying of another's ideas, was probably something neither eager Helen nor proud Annie worried about or even understood. On January 30, 1892, Helen wrote in her diary how her teacher "told me some very sad news which made me unhappy all day. Someone wrote Mr. Anagnos that the story which I sent him as a birthday gift, and which I wrote myself, was not my story at all, but that a lady had written it a long time ago. The person said her story was called 'Frost Fairies.' I am sure I never heard it. It made us feel so bad to think that people thought we had been untrue and wicked. My heart was full of tears, for I love the beautiful truth with my whole heart and mind."

Captain Keller quickly wrote to Anagnos that Helen "could not have received any idea of the story from any of her relatives or friends here, none of whom can communicate with her readily enough to impress her with the details of a story of that character. When Miss Annie first read it to us I questioned her closely about it and told her I did not think the dear child could have written it without suggestions from some older person, when she assured me that it was original as she now claims."

While his letter was meant to remove suspicion from his daughter and anyone else in the family, it certainly did not throw a favorable light on Annie. Even more damaging, however, was another Perkins teacher's testimony. This anonymous teacher reported to Anagnos her privately finger spelled conversation with Helen on February 22, while they were both sitting in the school parlor. "Did you ever write a story out of your own head?" she asked, noting that Helen's manner seemed "unmistakably troubled."

"Once I wrote a story King Frost from Frost King, but it was not exactly that," Helen replied.

"Someone read it to you?"

"Yes."

"Who?"

"Teacher."

"Last summer?"

"No, last fall."

"In the mountains?"

"No, in my own home."

Then Helen hurriedly confessed, "Teacher says I must not get mixed up, that Mrs. Hopkins read it to me when I was little."

Anagnos could hardly believe what he'd been told. How could Annie have lied to everyone and humiliate him in this way? Furiously, he stepped up the investigation and created a panel of four blind and four sighted teachers and officers of Perkins.

For two hours Helen was questioned. "The blood pressed about my thumping heart and I could scarcely speak except in monosyllables." When Helen left the room, she was dazed. That night she said she wept "as I hope few children have wept." Years later she recalled, "I felt so cold, I imagined I should die before morning, and the thought comforted me. I think if this sorrow had come to me when I was older, it would have broken my spirit beyond repairing."

Later the panel voted. Four said they thought Helen knew that the Canby story had been read to her; four voted Helen innocent. Anagnos voted "not proven," a kind of lukewarm defense of Helen and Annie. Soon afterward, he refused to support, mentor, or speak to Annie. His relationship with Helen ended, too.

Annie never forgave him.

What was undoubtedly most wrenching for Helen was having to back up Annie, who had been caught in her own lie. For someone like Helen, who had absolute faith in the truth, this experience must have been very traumatic. Creating a falsehood was something she was almost incapable of doing. "The deaf do not, because they cannot, deal in the nuances—particularly the verbal nuances—of personal relationships," explained David Wright, a deaf poet and writer from Britain. "Their dealings are direct—may appear outrageously direct: their handshakes are ungloved. They have a naïveté and also a plain honesty of intent, that often makes the polite wrappings-up of ordinary people seem, by contrast, hypocritical."

For Helen, this experience would have a lasting impact. "No child ever drank deeper of the cup of bitterness than I did. I had disgraced myself. I had brought suspicion upon those I loved best." In time, she came to believe that beloved Annie was the innocent victim and Anagnos was the villain. This was how she coped with the disturbing discovery that the one person in the world she depended on for almost all her information, mobility, and support might also do her harm.

In the spring of 1892, Helen and Annie left Perkins and returned to Tuscumbia. It was a humid, miserable summer. They spent part of the time at Fern Quarry, the family's rustic cabin in the mountains. Annie attempted to explain their exile in a letter to Bell's secretary, John Hitz, in November 1892: "Helen was very complaining. . . . The excitement of the last few weeks in Boston had overtaxed her strength; but we thought the pure mountain air and perfect quiet would soon restore her health and spirit. But the days passed and we failed to see any changes in her. She remained pale and listless—taking very little interest in her surroundings."

For a while that summer, Helen stopped reading. She stopped talking. She withdrew into her own world. The awkwardness, anger, moodiness, and restlessness on the surface may have been masking something happening beneath the surface: the beginning of her own adolescent struggle to figure out who she was, integrate her past and present, and find a place for herself in the world.

That summer Helen's confidence seemed badly shaken. While writing a letter or talking to someone, she would suddenly stop and finger-spell to Annie, "I am not sure it is mine." Annie tried to encourage her by suggesting she write another short article for *Youth's Companion* about the story of her life. Helen wrote with great hesitation and anxiety—an unpleasant process. After what must have been much prodding and scolding from her teacher, she began the piece with: "Written wholly without help of any sort by a deaf and blind girl, twelve years old . . . "

In 1893 Helen was blossoming into a lovely thirteen-year-old.

7.
A Widening Circle of Experience

It is the secret inner will that controls one's fate.
—Helen Keller, *The World I Live In*

$\mathcal{I}$N A PHOTOGRAPH TAKEN IN 1893, when Helen was thirteen, she sits in the usual right-faced profile in an angelic white dress with a high flouncy collar. Her brown hair falls in soft curls below her shoulders. She clutches a delicate spray of fragrant lilies of the valley and seems to gaze off into the distance with a slightly impish half-smile.

Somewhere hidden in this photograph is the Helen that she was becoming—in spite of all attempts to force her to remain as childlike as possible for as long as possible. Beneath her innocent outward appearance, Helen was beginning to make outrageous and rebellious requests. Recently, she had even announced to her startled family that she intended to go to college.

Little did Helen realize that young women were being warned to avoid "taxing brain work." S. Weir Mitchell, a respected Philadelphia neurologist and writer, exhorted girls that their "future womanly usefulness was endangered" if they read too much. Going to college, Weir claimed, ruined young women completely. A well-trained, middle-class young lady was expected to be "courteous, cheerful, polite, pious, moral, and benevolent." She had good table manners, showed respect for her parents, and was industrious and good-natured, according to H. Maria George in "Remarks on House-keeping" published in a popular magazine called *The Household* in 1880.

Not all girls during the Victorian era (1837–1901) made the transformation into proper young ladies willingly. As Frances E. Willard (1839–1898) woefully explained in her diary when she turned thirteen:

> This is my birthday and the date of my martyrdom. Mother insists that at last I *must* have my hair "done up woman-fashion." She says she can hardly forgive herself for letting me "run wild" so long. . . . My "back hair" is twisted up like a corkscrew; I carry 18 hair-pins; my head aches miserably; my feet are entangled in the skirt of my hateful new gown. I can never jump over a fence again, so long as I live.

For most proper, middle-class white girls, courtship started at age sixteen. Courting couples addressed each other as "Miss" and "Mister." Meetings between young men and women often took place in the parlor during piano duets or in croquet matches in the backyard. Eventually, these gave way to more public "dates": ice-skating or roller-skating (which gave couples a chance to hold hands in public) or going for a ride on one of the newfangled bicycles.

The average age for marriage in 1890 among young women was twenty-two. Young women were instructed in their behavior by etiquette books, religious tracts, and hygiene manuals, although a surprising number knew very little about reproduction even on the day of their marriages. Despite this fact, becoming a wife and a mother was every woman's goal.

A proper Victorian woman was given much contradictory advice. She was told that on her shoulders rested the power and responsibility to nurture her children, husband, and nation. At the same time she was characterized in the literature and speeches of the day as extremely fragile and prone to "hysteria and other nervous complaints." While reformers and physicians told young women to be healthy for the sake of their future children, another group of fashion advisers and etiquette experts urged them to look pale and delicate, to dress in tight-fitting whalebone corsets and suffocating, cumbersome dresses made from yards and yards of material.

While the rest of the girls Helen's age were looking forward to beginning courtship, thirteen-year-old Helen was completely ignorant of such romantic possibilities. It wasn't her fault. She could not readily compare herself with her contemporaries.

To make matters more confusing, her own mother was exceedingly prudish. She had already formed her own opinion about Helen's future. Because of Helen's disabilities, her mother decided, Helen must be kept safe from all young men. Ferociously protective Annie echoed such sentiments. Although Annie prided herself on her "liberal views," she carefully screened from Helen all disturbing ideas (such as death) or disturbing literature (such as the sensual poetry of Walt Whitman).

But neither her mother's caution nor her teacher's oversensitivity could prevent the inevitable.

Helen was growing up.

Helen reached her full height quickly. A Perkins report for 1891 described that she was of "symmetrical figure and weighs 122 pounds. . . . Her physique is magnificent. . . . Her head is finely formed, and decked with beautiful brown hair falling in luxuriant curls over her pretty shoulders." By age twelve she stood five feet two inches tall. She was changing inwardly as well as outwardly. "Is it not queer for a child to feel like laughing and crying all at once?" she wrote in a letter.

As Helen matured, Annie scrambled to find a new school and new patrons. Luckily, Bell stepped into the picture in 1892. His influence and power ultimately helped quell the rumors of the "Frost King" affair. He had other motives for helping Helen. He hoped to enlist Helen's fame to promote some of his ideas about deaf education.

In 1892 he published the *Helen Keller Souvenir*, a special issue of the *Volta Review*. This journal was one of the publications of the Volta Bureau, endowed with French prize money Bell had won for his invention of the telephone. The Volta Bureau was dedicated to "the increase and diffusion of knowledge relating to the deaf."

Generously, Bell whisked Annie and Helen to Niagara Falls in the summer of 1893 and then took them on an all-expense paid trip to the 1893 World's Columbian Exposition in Chicago. For three weeks they toured the fairgrounds of the White City, built to celebrate the discovery of the New World four hundred years ago.

Crowds stared at famous Helen as she roamed the exhibits with equally famous Dr. Alexander Graham Bell. Helen was given special permission to touch exhibits that ranged from bronze statues to rare diamonds. She refused, however, to inspect the Egyptian mummies. It must have been exhilarating for her to be surrounded by so many people, so many smells, so many sensations. She strolled the crowded fairground filled with the aroma of a newfangled caramel popcorn and peanut snack called Cracker Jack. She rode the amazing moving electric sidewalk and was carried 250 feet up into the air on the biggest Ferris wheel in the world. She encountered elephants, exotic dancers, Eskimos, and Japanese pagodas. In the Electrical Building she marveled at such wonders as telephones and phonographs.

While she was being challenged intellectually, she still had the same desires of a younger girl to have fun. One day Annie left Helen in the

Helen and Annie (front)
visited Niagara Falls with Edmund
Lyon and Polly Prate in 1893.

In July 1894 Helen and Annie visited with Bell during the Chautauqua, New York, meeting of the American Association to Promote Teaching of Speech to the Deaf.

hands of Carolyn Talcott, a young teacher at Rochester Institution who was attending a meeting for deaf teachers in Chicago. While Annie was gone, Helen and her new companion went for a visit to the exposition. "Miss Talcott," Helen asked, "is anybody watching us?"

No, Miss Talcott replied.

"Then let's romp."

For the next several months, Helen and Annie spent time in Tuscumbia and as guests at the home of wealthy benefactor William Wade in Hulton, Pennsylvania. It was not until the following summer of 1894 that Helen met John D. Wright and Dr. Thomas Humason while Annie gave a speech for deaf educators in Chautauqua, New York. Wright and Humason were starting a school in New York City to teach the deaf oral language. They promised that with their new methods, Helen could be taught to speak normally in no time.

Fourteen-year-old Helen was thrilled. At last she could continue regular schooling. In October 1894, she began classes at the Wright-Humason School, which was located near Central Park. It was a new beginning and she felt hopeful when she wrote to Caroline Derby, a friend from Boston, "I study Arithmetic, English Literature, and United States History. . . . I also keep a diary. I enjoy my singing lessons with Dr. Humason more than I can say." A few months later she wrote again to Caroline. The speech lessons were not going as well as she'd hoped.

Speech lessons were exhausting for someone with no sight. In spite of the difficulty and endless hours of practice, Helen did not give up. She was determined to learn to speak so that others could understand her.

Although Helen was surrounded by other deaf students her own age, she had surprisingly little direct communication with them. The Wright-Humason students were officially forbidden to learn or use sign language or finger spelling. Approaching Helen probably seemed daunting to the other students. Helen was different. She was the only blind-deaf student. And she was the only celebrity.

Helen maintained her good nature as she struggled to fit in. "We were such a rambunctious bunch of scapegraces—playing when we should work," she wrote years later, "spelling secretly when we should be improving our speech, making believe we were ill when it was time to go to church, and raising old Nick behind his [Mr. Wright's] back!"

She enjoyed walks in Central Park, hair-raising bobsled rides, and races on bridle paths on horseback, but at the point she needed and desired the company of girls her own age—she did not have much free and easy contact.

The friends Helen made were mostly older, wealthy men and women in New York City who befriended her and Annie. They included such luminaries as Clarence Stedman, a poet; Lawrence Hutton, writer, bibliophile, and wealthy man about town; Standard Oil executive Henry H. Rogers; and writer John Burroughs. One of Helen's favorites was writer Samuel Clemens, who also went by the name Mark Twain. Twain, almost sixty, was still recovering from the deaths of a son and daughter when Helen met him in 1894. Twain was fond of collecting what he called "angel fish," young girls whom he called his "grand daughters." Twain was especially moved by fourteen-year-old Helen, who reminded him of Joan of Arc, the subject of a book in progress.

Years later, Twain recalled the first time he saw Helen enter the room. "The girl began to deliver happy ejaculations, in her broken speech. Without touching anything, of course, and without hearing anything, she seemed quite well to recognize the character of her surroundings. She said, 'Oh, the books, the books, so many, many books. How lovely!'" Helen touched Twain's bristly white hair. She placed her fingers on his lips to lip-read his story. Twain, a humorist and superb performer, was uncharacteristically shy and embarrassed. When Annie asked him to tell Helen

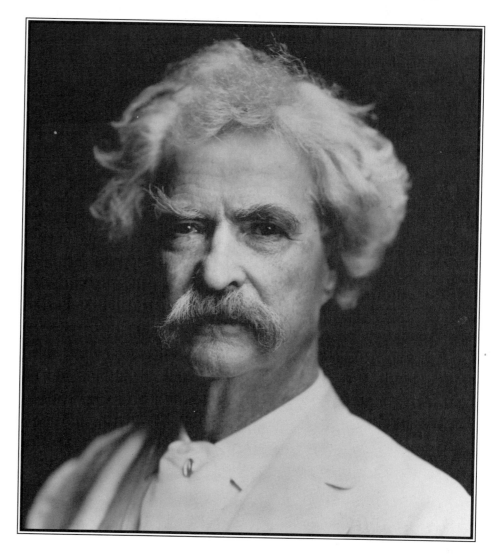

Mark Twain in 1907

some of his own experiences, he replied, "Oh, no, that would be too much like hell."

Helen later admitted that her strongest impression of Twain was that of sorrow. "There was about him the air of one who has suffered greatly. Whenever I touched his face his expression was sad, even when he was telling a funny story," wrote Helen. She and Annie spent time at Stormfield, Twain's home in Connecticut, where Helen appreciated most the fact that Twain was always a good listener. Twain treated her like a competent human being. Her last visit to Stormfield was in 1909, a few months before Twain's death. "He knew that we do not think with eyes and ears," she wrote, "and that our capacity for thought is not measured by five senses."

Money worries again began to plague Helen and Annie. In 1896, when Helen was sixteen, Helen's main benefactor, John P. Spaulding, the "sugar king" of Boston, died. No provision was made for Helen in his will. Helen and Annie were suddenly without financial support. Worse yet, Captain Keller had borrowed fifteen thousand dollars from Spaulding and now Spaulding's relatives wanted the money back.

Rich men and women were enlisted to support Helen's continuing education. Twain was among one of the most influential in organizing the seemingly boundless wealth (and guilt) that backed her scholarship funding. "It won't do for America," Twain wrote in a beseeching letter to Henry H. Rogers, Standard Oil magnate, "to allow this marvelous child to retire from her studies because of poverty. If she can go on with them she will make a fame that will endure in history for centuries. Along her special lines she is the most extraordinary product of all the ages."

Beginning in 1894 at Wright-Humason School and for the next several years as Helen managed to continue her studies, she spent more and more time away from home. She did not return to Tuscumbia for Christmas or summer holidays. Slowly, she drifted apart from her large, extended network of relatives and depended more and more on Annie as family. At the same time, Helen discovered that she did not fit in in Boston, New York, or Tuscumbia. This undoubtedly perplexed her as she grew into adolescence and found herself cut off from contact with her parents.

While Helen and Annie were busy in Massachusetts, Captain Keller died on August 19, 1896. Grief overwhelmed sixteen-year-old Helen. "My father is dead!" she wrote in a letter to Bell. "My own dear loving father! Oh, dear friend, how shall I bear it! . . . I never knew how dearly I loved my father until I realized that I had lost him."

Worse yet, when Helen tried to return to Tuscumbia for the funeral, her mother told her not to come. The heat, she said, was too intense. Helen felt heartbroken and rejected.

To deal with this tragedy, Helen turned to a new religious philosophy that she had been introduced to by John Hitz, Bell's secretary. These were writings by an eighteenth-century Swedish philosopher, mystic, and scientist, Emanuel Swedenborg. Swedenborg wrote extensively about universal brotherhood of mankind and the immediate presence of a loving God. Helen found especially appealing Swedenborg's view of life in the spiritual world that would be free of all bodily limitations. Hitz, who had lost most of his hearing, could fluently finger-spell and write in Braille. Helen first met Hitz in 1893, when she was about thirteen. They discussed Swedenborg's work extensively.

Helen's growing interest in Swedenborg was one of her first completely independent moves away from her family and Annie. Like so many adolescents, Helen was struggling to figure out how she fit into the universe. With help from Hitz, who provided her with Braille-embossed books by Swedenborg, she was able to carve out her own understanding separate from what was going on around her. Swedenborg's philosophy was considered fairly unusual—very different from the Presbyterian Church of her father, the staunch Episcopal Church of her mother, or the agnostic beliefs of Annie, who frankly told Helen she "had no faith in religion."

Although Helen never became a member of a particular Swedenborgian church, she would maintain faith in this philosophy throughout her life. "I do not know whether I adopted the faith or the faith adopted me," Helen later wrote in *My Religion*. "I can only say that the heart of the young girl sitting with a big book of raised letters on her lap in the sublime sunshine was thrilled by a radiant presence and inexpressibly endearing voice."

Helen and Annie on May 10, 1893

8.

A Dream and a Challenge

She ceased to teach me as a child, she did not command
me anymore.

—Helen Keller, *Teacher*

$\mathcal{I}$N 1896, AFTER TWO YEARS at the Wright-Humason School, it was
Annie, not Helen, who became impatient for a change. "I feel restive
under the school routine," Annie confided in a letter to Hitz. "You may
say what you will. I was never cut out for a schoolmarm." Annie was now
playing second fiddle to the teaching staff. She regularly criticized their
"stupidities" and their students' "plodding pursuit of knowledge." Just as
she had at Perkins, Annie began to create enemies.

When it appeared that Helen's speech was not improving in the way
that everyone had promised, Annie used this as an excuse to pull her out
of the school. She announced that they were beginning the advanced
studies Helen would need to take entrance exams for college.

Annie packed up Helen and left New York for Boston, where she had
plans for Helen to begin work at the Cambridge School for Young Ladies
in October 1896. Helen's dream was originally to go to Harvard. But
since the school did not allow women, her second choice was Radcliffe,
one of only a handful of colleges in the country devoted solely to women.

This was a bold, unusual move. No blind and deaf individual had ever successfully attended college before—much less a blind and deaf woman.

Helen hoped to fulfill a dream. For Annie, the decision to attempt what seemed the impossible—getting Helen ready for college—was a professional and personal challenge. At last she'd be able to prove to the world that she was not a "fraud or a humbug." Successfully getting Helen through college entrance exams would be a reflection on her own skills as a teacher. She agreed with the Cambridge School director, Arthur Gilman, that it would probably take Helen five years to prepare for college.

On the first day that Helen and Annie arrived at Cambridge School for Young Ladies, they sat in the parlor waiting to speak to Gilman. Helen ran her hands over the shelves to inspect the leather-bound spines and embossed titles of books lined up in a row. To her dismay, she discovered that the books were actually imitations, only parlor decorations. Her experience with the hearing and sighted girls at Cambridge would be an equally disappointing experience.

Helen was sixteen years old and yet this was her first experience of going to class and having daily contact with "normal" girls her own age. She soon became painfully aware that she was an outsider. The only way she could speak to most of the other girls was through Annie, who translated their chatter into finger spelling. This certainly must have dampened any secret-sharing or spontaneous jokes.

As she had at the Wright-Humason School, Helen tried to be a good sport. "I joined them in many of their games, even blind man's bluff and frolics in the snow," Helen later remembered. "I took long walks with them; we discussed our studies." A few of the girls learned to finger-spell so that they could talk to her directly. Most girls who were intimidated by her fame or were uncomfortable with her disability simply avoided her.

From January until June 1897, eleven-year-old Mildred Keller received a scholarship to take classes at Cambridge during Helen's second year there. With her sister's arrival, Helen's possibility for intimacy with the other students became even more remote. Her younger sister, who was among a handful of people who easily understood Helen's voice, con-

*Mildred Keller, Helen's sister, attended
the Cambridge School for Young Ladies
with her in 1897.*

sumed much of her attention. "For six happy months," Helen wrote of
her sister, "we were hardly ever apart."

Studies were difficult for Helen and for Annie, who had to finger-spell
most of the lectures and books. There were few textbooks available in
Braille. Few teachers knew finger spelling. Only her German teacher and
Gilman learned finger spelling well enough to give Helen instructions

directly. Helen could not make notes in class or write exercises. The sole way she could translate her thoughts to paper was through her manual Braille typewriter.

In spite of these incredible obstacles and the fact that no one on the staff had ever tried to teach a deaf-blind student before, Helen passed nine of the sixteen hours of preliminary examinations necessary for entrance into Radcliffe after her first year at Cambridge. She took these tests, which included elementary and advanced German, French, Latin, English, and Greek and Roman history, during the summer of 1897. She was especially pleased to have received honors in German and English.

While Helen's intellect was flowering, her beauty had blossomed, too. At age seventeen she was interviewed by a reporter, who noted how she fit the feminine ideal of the time. He described her as "a handsome, well-formed, graceful girl. The waist of her dress fits loosely, and there are not suggestions of corsets or of tight bands around the young girl's waist or neck." Her chief assets, according to this observer, were her pale delicate hands and her short brown curly hair. Her chin he described as "beautifully formed, her mouth and teeth are good, her complexion is clear and healthy."

At this point, Annie made a serious mistake in judgment. Emboldened by Helen's success, she decided it would be impressive to the many out-siders watching Helen's progress to speed up the remainder of her college preparatory work. Instead of five years, why not have Helen ready to enter Radcliffe in three?

Helen's work in the second year was to focus on mathematics, something that Annie had not taught her well because it was a subject she detested. Helen had developed her own mental block. She considered her-self a poor math student. It wasn't long before she began to buckle under so much stress. Her grades plummeted. Her self-confidence vanished. "Sometimes," she later wrote, "I lost all courage and betrayed my feelings in a way I am ashamed to remember."

Annie was a taskmaster and demanded perfection. She refused to give up the idea of Helen's accelerated program. But the other teachers at Cambridge began to worry about Helen's health. On November 12, after an especially difficult time with geometry, and what Annie called "natural causes" (Helen's menstrual period), Helen was sent to bed to rest.

An old friend, Mrs. Hopkins, arrived for a visit. Hopkins took one look at Helen and told Gilman that she was alarmed to find Helen in "a state of collapse." She went on to say that Helen was "more entirely cut off from intercourse with young people than she has ever been in her life and she is not happy. She told me that she missed the girls sadly, and in a very pathetic way added, but I have teacher and sister and ought to be happy."

Gilman wrote to Helen's mother that Helen's health demanded "an immediate change" in her workload. Even Helen's financial sponsors wrote notes to Annie. "Don't be too ambitious for her," wealthy dilettante Eleanor Hutton advised. However, instead of considering any of this advice, Annie only dug in harder and refused to budge. Finally, by appealing directly to Helen's mother, Gilman received a letter giving him authority to cut geometry and astronomy from her schedule.

Annie threatened to take Helen out of the school. She began a campaign of openly criticizing the other teachers. The matter finally reached a head on December 8, when Kate Keller, distressed by reports from various sources about Helen's health, authorized Gilman to act as her guardian and separate her and Mildred from Annie. According to Gilman, it had actually been Captain Keller's wish before he died "to remove Helen from her teacher."

For Helen, who had been informed only of Annie's point of view and of her dissatisfaction with everything at Cambridge, the news came as a terrible shock. "The most dreadful sorrow burst upon us which we ever endured," Helen wrote on December 8. "Mr. Gilman, whom I had trusted, had done it all." She and her sister were badly shaken.

Once the sponsors of Helen's education found out that Annie was to be removed, they protested loudly. Annie stomped out of the school. "We both felt so badly at having Miss Annie go away, that we couldn't keep from crying all day," Mildred later wrote.

Annie sent a telegram to Helen's mother with only three words: "We need you." When their mother arrived and found both girls in good health but hysterical, she changed her mind. Perhaps the idea of being completely responsible for Helen seemed overwhelming to her. "Very soon the injustice of [my decision] overcame me," she later wrote. "I found that Mr. Gilman had made a cruel use of the authority I had given him to distress my children. . . . I certainly never dreamed of Miss Sullivan being forced away from Helen."

Neither Helen nor her sister returned to Cambridge. Once again, Helen assumed Annie's version of what happened to be the truth. She was cut off from the support she needed to complete her education and was once more set adrift. What would she do now? Where would she go?

Fortunately, a friend opened his home and hospitality to Helen and Annie. They were invited to stay with Ed Chamberlin (whom Helen called "Uncle Ed") and his family at Red Farm near Wrentham, Massachusetts, for the next several months. A tutor was hired to meet weekly with Helen for lessons.

While at Wrentham, Annie became depressed. During her terrible dark moods, she would disappear for hours. Sometimes she hid under an overturned boat or trudged into the woods alone and refused to speak to Helen or anyone else. A sensitive teenager, Helen admitted that she "occasionally felt alone and bewildered by some of her peculiarities . . .

RED FARM, WRENTHAM.

Red Farm in Wrentham, Massachusetts, was the place where Helen spent many happy days with the Chamberlin family in 1897.

the strangeness was there. Something too subtle for words was lacking in our relations to each other. . . . ”

Helen once described Annie as a "web of flame." Her teacher's moods were unpredictable, ill-timed, and often caught innocent bystanders unaware. While Annie might be filled with anger or melancholy one minute, she could just as easily laugh and joke and act particularly loving the next. She had two very different sides to her personality.

One of Helen's nightmares during this time of her life illustrated the anguish and confusion she felt toward her unpredictable teacher: "Although I have the strongest, deepest affection for my teacher, yet when she appears to me in my sleep, we quarrel and fling the wildest reproaches at each other," Helen wrote. "She seizes me by the hand and drags me by main force [toward] I can never decide what—an abyss, a perilous mountain pass, or a rushing torrent, whatever in my terror I may imagine."

Helen at eighteen was struggling with her own identity, separate from her teacher or her mother. In diary entries during the spring of 1898 she revealed wildly swinging emotions. On March 11 she recorded a "perfectly wonderful day," a drive in the country "full of fragrant messages of coming spring." Then, eleven days later, she wrote on March 22: "Tonight I'm having a hard fight with—I don't know what—myself or some bad fairy that doesn't love me. I haven't done well in Algebra, and my temper has been unmanageable. I am usually willing to persevere, but I wouldn't today because I was treated so much like—well—a naughty child."

At one point during the spring, when the country entered the war with Spain, Annie made a bizarre announcement. She suddenly decided she should go to Cuba to volunteer as a nurse. Perhaps it was uncertainty about the future, her failing eyesight, or Helen's own rebelliousness that prompted the decision. By the end of the spring, Annie had given up on the idea of becoming a nurse. Her depression ended.

The summer Helen turned eighteen she longed for independence as an adult but at the same time resisted leaving her long childhood behind. For someone with as much energy as Helen, conforming to the ideal of a "proper" young lady could be a severe trial. On a cool, breezy day in early

July, her thirteen-year-old sister, Mildred, "the perfect child" who was quickly becoming a perfect young lady, came for a visit to Red Farm with their mother.

On a morning hike through the woods, Helen, Mildred, and some of the other rambunctious young people made a game of pushing one another off the trail. They hooted, hollered, crossed the field, and hurled themselves into a pile of hay. The dog jumped on them and barked. On the way through the woods, Helen and the others kept falling down and "disentangling ourselves from briars and small trees."

Helen and the others thought the situation very funny and laughed and laughed. Mildred was not amused by such wild childish antics.

In the midst of so much chaos and change, Helen again turned to her religion. John Hitz, the ready listener, corresponded with her regularly in letters. More and more, this philosophy had appeal for idealistic Helen, who saw life as unambiguous: black and white, evil and good.

Helen wrote a letter to Hitz explaining how the philosophy of Swedenborg made her feel as if she had been "restored to equality with those who have all their faculties." Helen admitted that life wasn't easy. "I feel weary of groping, always groping along the darkened path that seems endless. At such times the desire for the freedom and the larger life of those around me is almost agonizing. But when I remember the truths you have brought within my reach, I am strong again and full of joy."

Helen seemed to find happiness and a kind of new inner strength as well. At Red Farm, she wrote in her diary, "I seem to laugh more all the time . . . and I get happier and happier." The farm was the meeting place for many different writers and poets who discussed politics. Uncle Ed spoke to Helen as if she were a grown-up person. He discussed history and introduced her to the poetry of Walt Whitman, which prim Annie thought too disgusting to share. For Helen, the months at Red Farm were "the richest, brightest experience of our lives."

Years later, Helen spoke of this crucial turning point in her relationship with Annie. It was after their time at Red Farm that her teacher finally "ceased to teach me as a child, she did not command me anymore." What exactly prompted Annie's realization that she could no longer treat Helen like a child? Perhaps it was because Helen herself stubbornly resisted Annie's often heavy-handed, critical techniques. Helen had finally begun to formulate her own identity, her own religious views, her own ideas about where she fit into the universe.

In the autumn of 1898 Helen and Annie moved into a boardinghouse in Boston near the home of her new tutor, Merton S. Keith. Helen missed Red Farm, she wrote to Eleanor Hutton, but she said that "I have the certainty that something sweet and good will come to me in this great city where human beings struggle so bravely all their lives to wring happiness from cruel circumstances. Anyway I am glad to have my share in life whether it be bright or sad."

Helen had survived cruel circumstances. She was now ready—and able—to handle happiness.

Helen at Radcliffe in 1904 enjoyed the companionship of her Boston terrier, Phiz.

9.

"To Be Myself"

I felt that all the forces of my nature were cudgelling me
to college.

—Helen Keller, "An Apology for Going to College,"
McClure's Magazine, 1905

In September 1900 Helen entered Radcliffe as a freshman. She was
twenty years old and filled with energy to meet and discuss heady philosophy with girls who were "interested in the same subjects I was, and who
were trying like me to hew out their own paths in life." For the second
time in her life, she would be surrounded by hearing and sighted young
women. No one blind or deaf had ever attended Radcliffe.

After the Civil War, Radcliffe was one of only a half-dozen colleges
opened exclusively for women on the East Coast. By the eve of the twentieth century, more and more land grant colleges in the Midwest and West
were making a college education available to women as well as men. And
yet, even as more women were attending college, the idea still irked many
Americans. They worried that too much education would harm women
and make them mannish, disagreeable, and perhaps even insane.

"I knew that there would be obstacles to conquer," Helen wrote, "but
they only whetted my desire to try my strength by the standards of normal
students."

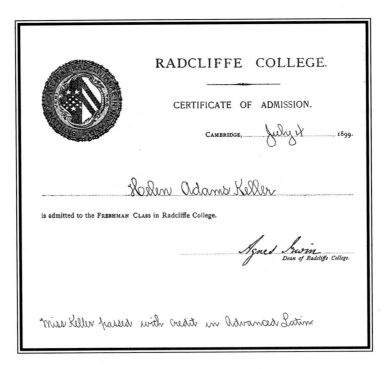

*Helen's certificate of admission to Radcliffe opened new doors
for her quest for knowledge.*

Once again, however, Helen was disappointed. The professors kept their distance and seemed to her "as impersonal as Victrolas." Only one of her teachers bothered to learn the manual alphabet so that he could talk directly to her. Most discouraging of all, Helen found she had little in common with the other young women. She was still an outsider. It didn't help that Annie insisted they live off-campus in a small rented house—a location that provided even fewer opportunities for Helen to meet or eat with the other students. Occasionally she would join in hikes through the woods, sleigh rides, and popcorn parties around a fire. She liked to go rowing, horseback riding, and sailing. But there was little time for much recreation.

The other women at Radcliffe probably did not know what to make of Helen. She was the first blind and deaf person many of them had ever met. Her fame made her seem distant. Encounters were often awkward. It was nearly impossible for a student who was not an outsider to imagine what it must have been like to be an outsider. The idea was probably terrifying.

As days passed, Helen admitted that her dreams began to fade into a "rather drab reality." She did not make the new friends she had imagined.

In fact, only one of the young women learned to speak to Helen directly. In the lunchroom the friendlier or more curious students gathered around her and ate their sandwiches and eclairs. As usual, it was Annie who spelled "their bright chatter" into Helen's hand. Helen knew that her friendships depended on people learning the manual alphabet. The girls "could not reach me through my isolation, and in the midst of my class I could not help at times feeling lonely and sad."

The students elected Helen the vice president of the class, but she had little time to enjoy any camaraderie or fun that the job might have entailed. She had to study constantly to keep up. Perhaps out of a sense of guilt or well-meaning generosity, a group of girls gave Helen a Boston terrier. She named him Phiz. He would be the first of many dogs she would keep as pets as an adult. "I loved their affectionate ways and the eloquent wags of their tails," Helen wrote. But what she wanted was not the companionship of an "honest, homely Boston terrier." What she wanted was the companionship of other people her own age.

Helen, Annie, and Phiz climbed a tree to read a book during endless studies at Radcliffe.

Helen felt as if her college experience was too hurried, "like rushing through Europe on a summer holiday." All the subjects she longed to linger over—literature, philosophy—she could examine only in fleeting glimpses. Few of her course books were available in Braille. Most of the required reading had to be read to her by Annie, who spelled the entire text into her hand. While everyone else was sleeping, Helen and Annie struggled to keep up with the day's assignment.

With Annie's limited educational background, she made constant use of dictionaries in English, German, and Latin. Her sight was beginning to fail, and Helen's own health was beginning to suffer under the extreme workload. She suffered from headaches but refused to tell any doctor for fear that Annie would be accused of overworking her. Helen became anemic after periodically refusing to eat.

Radcliffe made no special effort to help Helen succeed. In fact, the staff was not especially pleased to have Helen as a student. Some instructors complained that Annie might cheat for Helen. As a result, all of Helen's tests were carefully given to Helen in Braille with Annie out of the room.

College did open important windows for Helen. She discovered philosophers like Socrates, Plato, and Descartes who "waked something in me that has never slept since." Through a beloved composition teacher, Charles Townsend Copeland, she had her first taste of truly helpful feedback about her writing. Most important, she began to accept herself the way she was. She vowed to make her own observations about life in her own unique way. As she explained to Copeland:

> When I came to your class last October, I was trying with all my might to be like everybody else, to forget as entirely as possible my limitations' peculiar environment. Now, however, I see the folly of attempting to hitch one's wagon to a star that does not belong to it. . . . Henceforth I am resolved to be myself, to live my own life, and write my own thoughts when I have any.

This was something of a declaration of independence coming from someone who had spent almost all her life trying to please the hearing and seeing people around her.

John Hitz (top right), seated beside Helen, introduced her to Swedenborgianism. Alexander Melville Bell (Top left), the inventor's father, Annie, and Alexander Graham Bell (kneeling) enjoyed a breezy summer holiday at Bell's house in Nova Scotia in 1901.

In 1901, at the end of Helen's freshman year, she and Annie spent time in Nova Scotia at Dr. Bell's summer home with his family and friends. Bell was well aware that Helen had not spent much time with any young men her own age. He made a special point of taking her aside and privately telling her, "Your limitations have placed you before the world in an unusual way. You have learned to speak, and I believe you are meant to break down the barriers which separate the deaf from mankind. There are unique tasks waiting for you, a unique woman."

For Helen, nearly twenty-one and not yet graduated, Bell's words must have seemed a little overwhelming. As he continued, she began to squirm.

"It seems to me, Helen, a day must come when love, which is more than friendship, will knock at the door of your heart and demand to be let in."

Bell encouraged her not to think that just because she was blind and deaf that she was "debarred from the supreme happiness of woman. Heredity is not involved in your case, as it is in so many others."

Helen protested, saying she was happy with her teacher and mother and interesting work to do. "I really don't care a bit about being married."

He cautioned that one day her mother might die, her teacher might marry, "and there may be a barren stretch in your life when you will be very lonely."

"I can't imagine a man wanting to marry me. I should think it would seem like marrying a statue."

"You are very young," he said and gave her hand a pat. "If a good man should desire to make you his wife, don't let anyone persuade you to forgo that happiness because of your peculiar handicap."

Helen began her second year of college. One morning in the autumn of 1901, Helen was unexpectedly called out of her Latin class to meet with editor William Alexander of the *Ladies' Home Journal*. He was interested in publishing, in five monthly installments, the story of her life. He promised to pay her $3,000. Helen was filled with happiness. For the first time she would be earning money on her own. "In my imagination the story was

Helen as a Radcliffe student and Bell in 1902

John Macy in 1900

already written. Indeed it had already found a sure place in 'The Golden Treasury of Literature.' My happiness and conceit knew no bounds."

The reality of actually coming up with the required material was a lot more work than Helen had anticipated. After she used up all the available themes from Copeland's class, she admitted feeling "in deep water and frightened out of my wits." Publisher's letters began to arrive thick and fast demanding the next chapter. Telegrams stated flatly: "There is not a connection between page six and seven. Wire the missing part."

Fortunately, a friend put Helen and Annie in touch in 1902 with John Albert Macy, a twenty-five-year-old Harvard English instructor and editor of *Youth's Companion*. After learning the manual alphabet, he helped her edit the remaining articles and put them together in a book, *The Story of My Life*, which was published in 1903 by Doubleday. The book was Helen's first full-length writing project. Although the book sold about ten thousand copies the first year, it remained in print and slowly became a kind of classic—no small achievement for someone still in college.

"I liked him," Helen wrote of Macy. "He was eager, intelligent, gentle." She thought of him as "a friend, a brother, and an advisor all in one." For Helen he was a kind of "knight errant" who delivered her from her problems with writing her book and then went on to create a wonderful friendship. His editorial assistance proved to be invaluable.

Writing did not come easily for Helen, who often found the process slow-going and tedious. "Sometimes I feel ideas beating against my brain like caged birds; but they will not sing themselves in words, at least not yet," she confessed. "It seems as if everything one would care to say, had been said by somebody else." She described writing as "agonizing" and often felt a kind of physical discomfort "caused by the sense of wasted time and the harrowing uncertainty of the result."

One difficulty was that Helen had to create in one language (Braille), translate her words into another (typewritten English), and then, when the editing process began, have the words translated back again through finger spelling—all the time trying to create a unified whole.

Helen's amazing memory came in handy. Heaps of papers, some in Braille, some typewritten, some merely scraps of notes, were spread all over the floor. These had been created sporadically by Helen and had to be put together to make a whole. "She remembered whole passages, some of which she had not seen for many weeks, and could tell, before Miss Sullivan had spelled into her hand a half-dozen words of the paragraphs under discussion, where they belonged and what sentences were necessary to make the connections clear," Macy wrote.

He was impressed by her dogged determination. "Labor is the content of Miss Keller's genius, the secret of her advancement. Not a good paragraph which she has written, even in a private letter, has been 'dashed off.' . . . She writes well not by virtue of a facile gift, but by scrupulous revision, patient thinking, and diligent attention to the criticism of her instructors."

Macy was a brilliant editor and a gifted writer. Tall and charming, he liked to consider himself something of a revolutionary. He mingled with socialist poets and writers and American communists. He introduced Helen to a variety of literature and ideas she never would have discovered at Radcliffe or under the rather conservative outlook of Annie. He kept her in touch with current events. If he discovered a book he liked, he'd read it to Helen or have it made into Braille. Through him she discovered the science fiction of H. G. Wells, novels by Leo Tolstoy, and the political writings of Karl Marx.

Macy was enchanted with both Helen and Annie, who was thirty-six years old when he began working with Helen. He described Annie, who was almost eleven years older than he was, as "independent and willful as

Helen, Annie, and John in 1914

her pupil, of vigorous personality." She may have reminded him of his short, ambitious mother, whom he worshipped and described as "a midget of courage." At this point Annie's eyesight was failing, and she was also having trouble walking. She was becoming portly and matronly looking. But Macy was infatuated with her. "She has humor, buoyancy, exhaustless nervous energy," he wrote of Annie in an article called "Helen Keller As She Really Is."

Helen, three years younger than Macy, was quite stunning. He described her as "tall and strongly built, always had good health. She seems to be more nervous than she really is because she expresses more with her hands than do most English-speaking people." He admired her habit of mind of doing everything "thoroughly and well." He was also impressed by her physical bravery. She had, he said, "a boy's contempt for the fellow who cries." When she went hiking in the woods and plunged through the underbrush and became scratched and bruised, "you could not get her to admit she was hurt, and you certainly could not persuade her to stay at home next time."

Helen's humor charmed him. "If she doesn't know the answer to a question," he said, "she guesses with mischievous assurance."

When Helen needed to remember something she "fluttered it off swiftly on the fingers of her right hand." Sometimes her finger-play was unconscious. She talked to herself absentmindedly in manual alphabet. "When she is walking up and down the hall or along the veranda, her hands go flying along beside her like a confusion of bird's wings."

Helen's face was animated when she spoke. When someone else spoke, her hand would go automatically to that person's face to examine what she called "the twist of mouth," the subtle expression revealed in the set of the jaw. This was how she understood tone.

Helen could not have mistaken the growing attraction between Macy and her teacher. Annie's romance was something completely new and baffling for her. She liked to describe Macy's "brotherly tenderness, fine sensibilities, keen sense of humor." She felt they were a well-matched couple because of their intelligence and wit. Macy's arrival on the scene also solved a problem for Annie. As Helen neared graduation, it was clear that there would be little more for Annie to do.

In 1903, before Helen's official graduation, Helen and Annie had enough money to buy a "small, old farmhouse, long and narrow and decidedly Puritanical," surrounded by seven neglected acres and a barn in Wrentham. The property cost $2,700. They used the money from Helen's articles, book, and some stock given to them by Boston philanthropist John S. Spaulding.

Helen had high hopes for the property and planned to renovate the place so that it would one day be like her father's farm in Tuscumbia. She was thrilled to have the farmhouse's two pantries converted into her study. She even had her own door that permitted her to go outside and stand and smell a cluster of pines. Macy created a long wire around the property that allowed Helen to go for a quarter-mile walk by herself. "The house is on one of the prettiest village streets, and has trees around it," Helen wrote Hitz. "Is it not lovely to look forward to living in a home of our own and doing just as we like?"

What Helen did not mention was that she still wasn't sure what she wanted to do when she graduated. The *Ladies' Home Journal* paid her to write about her plans in an article, "My Future As I See It." She mentioned possibly teaching—perhaps she'd help other afflicted children. She considered writing or translating classics. In the Radcliffe yearbook, her picture was printed next to the prediction: "H. K. missionary?" Another student wrote a poem dedicated to Helen:

> *Beside her task our efforts pale,*
> *She never knew the word for fail;*
> *Beside her triumphs ours are naught,*
> *For hers were far more dearly bought.*

In spite of upbeat comments from classmates and editors, Helen was secretly filled with anxiety about what she would do with the rest of her life.

Helen graduated from Radcliffe in 1904.

10.

Breaking New Ground

I resolved that whatever role I did play in life it would
not be a passive one.

—Helen Keller, *Midstream*

$\mathcal{L}$IBERATED YOUNG WOMEN LIKE Helen who had broken the barriers and
gone to college faced uncertain futures. "They suddenly found themselves
not merely alone, but alone in a society that had no use for them," wrote
historian William O'Neill. Educated women in the United States had limited professional opportunities open to them outside of teaching. In 1900
there were a total of only 208 female lawyers and 4,557 female doctors in
the United States. Women could not vote. Once married, they could not
own property on their own. As a college-educated woman who also happened to be blind and deaf, Helen faced what seemed to be almost insur-
mountable prejudice.

The prospect of graduation proved to be traumatic for Annie as well.
Her health began to break down. What would she do now that Helen's
education was almost "finished"? Annie never seriously pursued teaching
beyond her work with Helen. She never took up Bell's idea of starting a
school for the deaf or blind. She did not have the discipline to write for a
living, although she was a talented writer when she wanted to work at it.
Her life as well as Helen's seemed at sea.

On June 28, 1904, when Helen had just turned twenty-four, she sat on the stage in the crowded, stuffy Sanders Theater with ninety-five other graduates. In Radcliffe's twenty-five-year history, this was the biggest graduating class. Annie and John Hitz were in the audience. Helen's mother did not attend because of illness.

When it came time for Helen to receive her diploma, she gracefully went up the steps with Annie, who had attended every class with her for the past four years. The audience applauded politely. It is impossible to say if Annie betrayed her own disappointment that Helen had graduated "cum laude," with honors, but not "summa cum laude"—highest honors. As soon as the ceremony ended, Annie and Helen slipped out the door before any curious well-wishers could swarm around them.

Later that fall, Helen did not have such good luck avoiding her growing number of fans. In October 1904 she and Annie and John Macy went to St. Louis to attend the Louisiana Purchase Exposition. October 18 had been declared Helen Keller Day. Crowds jammed Congress Hall, where educators and others were gathering to hear and see Helen Keller herself. Spectators had to be prevented from climbing through the windows on stepladders.

When Helen came into the hall, even the guards lost control of the mob. The crowd grabbed the roses Helen was carrying and snatched the hat off her head for souvenirs. She managed to push her way to the platform to speak. For once, her articulation was fairly clear. Then someone hoisted onto a table twin boys, both blind, who played the violin badly. Even so, some people in the crowd were reported to be sobbing with emotion.

The entire affair was disappointing for Helen, who had hoped to create some interest specifically in the plight faced by the blind and deaf. Somehow her "luminous presence," as one blind spectator called it, had worked some other kind of magic on the crowd. All anyone could think about or talk about was the marvelous Helen Keller, the miracle.

In spite of her growing fame, Helen still didn't know what she wanted to do with her life. How would she be able to support herself? "I asked myself how I could use the education I was receiving. I felt that there must be some particular task for me, but what was it?" Meanwhile, friends were busy making plans for her. Some suggested she start a special school for "afflicted children." The queen of Romania, who wanted to start a place for the blind to live and work, became incensed when Helen refused to help her. Helen believed strongly that the handicapped should not be separated from the rest of the population. The queen never spoke to her again.

In May 1905 Annie Sullivan married John Macy at their Wrentham farmhouse. Only twenty guests attended, including Helen's mother, who approved of Macy's intelligence and "his wholesome presence." Before the wedding, she wrote to Macy, "It would have been too cruel if you had not loved Helen." Clearly, he knew what he was getting into. "He had married an institution, he knew that in the beginning," a friend wrote. "Helen came first. He was willing to have it so."

As soon as news reached Henry H. Rogers that Annie had a husband, he cut Helen's annuity in half, from one hundred dollars a month to fifty, expressing the Victorian idea that a man would contribute half of their income. Valiantly, Helen announced that she would "make enough with my pen to supply the deficiency." Helen would continue to live at Wrentham and do her share to keep the financial machinery moving.

Unfortunately, Annie did not have an outside income and Macy's money was quickly spent. "Financial difficulties have seemed nearly always an integral part of our lives," Helen later admitted. The stress of coming up with enough money would haunt them at Wrentham.

Yet in her later years Helen would always recall the early days of her teacher's marriage among the happiest and most productive of their lives. She and her teacher and Macy were busy with their work. Macy went to Boston to keep up with his editorial duties on *Youth's Companion*. Helen had magazine articles to finish, letters to write. She began *The World I Live In* as a challenge to show how she used her sense of touch, taste, and smell to understand her environment. This appeared first as a series of essays in *Century* magazine.

She enjoyed this project in a way she had not enjoyed any other writing she had done up till this point. In *The World I Live In*, which was published as a book in 1908, she attempted for the first time to bring the reader inside her own sensory experiences of touch, smell, and taste—senses that for most Americans were largely undeveloped or unrecognized. Helen shared

In 1914, when this photo was taken of Helen, Annie, John Macy, and Helen's dog Sieglinde at their home in Wrentham, the Macy marriage was about to end.

her experiences in a way that was surprising for many people who considered themselves "superior" because they could see and hear.

"Touch brings the blind many sweet certainties which our more fortunate fellows miss, because their sense of touch is uncultivated. When they look at things, they put their hands in their pockets. No doubt that is why their knowledge is often so vague, inaccurate, and useless."

For Helen, every atom of her body was a kind of vibroscope. She was not entombed in silence the way so many people liked to think. Instead, a whole array of sensations penetrated her skin, "the nerves, the bones," she wrote, "like pain, heat, and cold." For example, when she experienced a beating drum, the vibration "smites me through from the chest to the shoulder-blades."

Many readers were surprised to discover that Helen could identify a whole catalogue of jars and jolts: the *plop* of milk in a pitcher, the pop of a cork, the sputter of flame, the *tick-tock* of the clock, and "the deceptive tap of a breeze at the window and the door." She sensed "the whack of heavy falling bodies, the sudden shimmering splinter of chopped logs, the crystal shatter of pounded ice, the crash of a tree hurled to earth by a hurricane, the irrational persistent chaos of noise made by switching freight trains, the blasting of stone and the terrific grinding of rock . . . "

From her time at Wrentham, Helen knew by the insistent vibrations when someone was hammering or sawing nearby. She could tell from the slight flutter on the rug that a breeze had blown her papers off the table. A "round thump" meant a pencil was rolling on the floor; a flat thud indicated a fallen book. When Annie wanted her to come down for dinner, she made a wooden rap on the balustrade.

Once when she was sitting at the dinner table she began laughing. No one knew why. Only Helen sensed the vibrations of the stout maid in the kitchen performing a comical jig. "I sat still and listened with my feet," she wrote.

Helen could identify people and their ages by their footsteps on a bare floor. A young girl, she said, walked with a rapid, elastic rhythm. An elderly woman moved much more slowly in a faltering gait. Even the mood of the walker was revealed by the vibrations of their footsteps. "I feel in them firmness and indecision, hurry and deliberation, activity and laziness, fatigue, carelessness, timidity, anger, and sorrow."

From years of living with the mercurial temper of Annie, Helen had perfected the ability to follow the changes in moods and the sudden changes in action of people around her—when they sat, kneeled, or got up—from the certain jars and jerks in the vibrations through the floor. She could even pinpoint accurately the moment the dog jumped on the sofa when he wasn't supposed to.

Many things were revealed to Helen by placing her hands on a speaker's lips and throat. She could sense a boy's chuckle, a man's "whew!" of surprise. She sensed the "Ahem!" of annoyance or perplexity, the moan of pain, the choke of a sob.

When Helen walked around town, she knew where she was because each shop emanated a different odor. Likewise, she knew the occupation of the people she met from many distinct odors. She could tell if someone was a carpenter or an artist, a mason or a chemist, by the odors of wood, iron, paint, or drugs that clung to their clothing. Even people passing quickly by on the street left her with a "scent impression" of where they had been: the kitchen, the garden, the sickroom. She recognized acquaintances instantly by smell. One friend was surprised when she recognized him in person by matching the smell of tobacco from his letters.

The World I Live In, expertly edited by Macy, proved to be a revelation to many readers. To the Victorian sensibility, the blind-deaf lived a very different kind of existence, often described as a "dark pit" or "being buried alive." After the book's publication, publishers clamored for more of the same. The public's hunger for information about her unique experience proved insatiable.

While Helen was busy breaking new ground with her writing, Annie was feeling less than fulfilled. Her job was to help Helen. As household staff quit repeatedly, Annie found that she had to spend more and more time in the kitchen—a place she did not enjoy. Her moods began to swing wildly. One time she stomped away and rode off on a fast horse that threw her. Furious, Helen berated her for "mad escapades." Then, just as quickly as Annie's temper flared, it disappeared. She begged Helen for forgiveness. "I was trying to run away from the kitchen and everything that makes one old," she confessed.

It was impossible for either Annie or Macy, who was also a poet, to compete with Helen. Helen was the writer the magazines and publishers wanted. This created a growing tension. In 1909 Helen submitted a poem about the farm's stone wall. "As we laid one stone upon another," she wrote to Hitz, "I kept fingering the various shapes, textures, and sizes, and I became aware of a beauty in them that I had not sensed before." Fascinated by the history of the area, Helen convinced Macy to take her to the cemetery to touch the ancient tombstones and try to make out the inscriptions. The poem began: "O beautiful blind stones, inarticulate and dumb!" She sold "Song of the Stone Wall" for three hundred dollars.

Helen and Annie and Macy threw themselves into renovation of the farm—with disastrous results. They bought apple trees that were devoured by deer. They purchased horses that proved to be "wild, insane," and untrainable and chickens that immediately died. They took in dozens of ill-behaved pets, including a Great Dane that broke all the dishes and was "more like an elephant than a dog." All these costly investments plunged them deeper into debt.

Macy, who had always been a fairly heavy drinker, complained of being unable to pay his dues at the St. Botolph's Club, where he often went to meet his friends. He ran up other debts as well. The Macy marriage, which began as an idealistic partnership, soon soured. Arguments between Annie and Macy erupted with greater frequency.

Meanwhile, as Helen's fame continued to spread, she received more and more letters from people asking for her help. Some wanted her to help

Helen in 1907 was an accomplished horsewoman who often rode with Annie in Central Park.

sponsor fund drives. Others had plans for her to help blind institutions and deaf schools. She was badgered by callers with all kinds of far-fetched schemes. Throughout this time, Helen struggled to maintain some sense of her own identity. "All through my life," she later wrote, "people who imagine themselves more competent than my teacher and I have wanted to organize my affairs. . . . They assured us that if we followed their plan, we should win fame and fortune, and incidentally benefit some good cause. They talked, they wrote, they brought their friends to help them, and went away, and the next day others came."

Helen found these demands intrusive. She was a natural at raising funds for causes she believed in. When she was only ten, she single-handedly spearheaded a campaign to raise money to pay the tuition for a motherless blind-deaf boy, five-year-old Tommy Stringer, so that he could attend Perkins Institution. While still in college, she first "heard the call of the sightless" and in 1903 joined an association formed by the Women's Education and Industrial Union in Boston to promote the welfare of the adult blind. Helen appeared before the legislature to plead the case that the blind needed work and asked for a state commission to be set up.

Helen discovered she was good at this kind of work, yet wondered how she could make a living at it. In 1906 she was appointed by the governor of Massachusetts to attend sessions of the Massachusetts Commission for the Blind. Helen sensed her own limitations, unable to make herself be understood. Because all conversation had to be finger-spelled rapidly by Annie, she felt chagrined when she couldn't keep up or speak out against points being presented. Finally, she quit and decided to improve her speech so that she would be able to participate fully.

In 1907, Helen wrote a pathbreaking article for the *Ladies' Home Journal* in an effort to prevent needless ophthalmia neonatorum, blindness among infants. Since 1881, the medical profession had known that nearly two-thirds of the blind children entering school were afflicted with this disease, which they received at birth because of a germ that attacked the eyes. The germ was caused by venereal disease, something no proper Victorian women's magazines dared mention. Yet the cure was simple—treating the child's eyes at birth with a cleansing solution. Helen wrote several articles on the subject and helped rally forces to convince the medical establishment to make such steps a regular part of procedures in hospitals.

Helen was appalled to discover that there was no unified clearinghouse of information for the blind. No one in America had ever made an accurate census of the country's blind or their occupations. No one knew what anyone else was doing in schools and societies for the blind. Few Braille books were available at reasonable costs. To make matters worse, no unified Braille style existed in printed books. Five different kinds of Braille type existed, which made the blind person's task of learning to read even more difficult.

Helen worked to support one Braille style. She also was surprised to discover "a medieval ignorance concerning the sightless," and worked tirelessly to help adults who became blind late in life, when it was too late to go to school or learn a new job skill. The blind were seldom found doing things they would like most to do or were best at doing.

Slowly, Helen discovered as she corresponded with many people around the world that she had a talent for making the sighted understand the special difficulties faced by the blind and deaf. It was a tough choice to pick one disability on which to focus her efforts. "Although I was as deeply interested in the cause of the deaf as I was in that of the blind and had always thought deafness before acquisition of language a greater affliction than blindness," Helen admitted, "I found it was not humanly possible to work for both the blind and deaf at the same time."

Helen's life at Wrentham was full and strenuous. "Often we would leave home with all the housework undone, hasten to a meeting, go through with its inevitable tiresome social functions, and return to Wrentham to find fresh tasks added to our already heavy burden."

Helen did what she could to help with the housework. She cleared the table, washed the dishes, and tidied up the rooms. Meanwhile, letters poured in, articles and books clamored to be written. "But home was home, and somebody had to make the beds, pick the flowers, start the windmill and stop it when the tank was filled, and be mindful of the little almost unnoticed things which constitute the happiness of family life," Helen wrote.

Several times, the three of them tried in their idealistic way to "barricade" themselves to live a simple life without interruptions. They never succeeded. "In spite of our attempted hermit life," she admitted, "we were imperatively called out to new duties."

One thing that could not be barricaded from their life was the need for money. Helen tried her hand at writing different kinds of articles but soon discovered that all the public wanted her to write about was herself or the blind. When she wrote about other topics that she felt passionate about—politics, current affairs, or Shakespeare—magazines turned her down.

Once again Helen found herself at a crossroads.

"I felt the tide of opportunity rising and longed for a voice that would be equal to the urge that was sweeping me out into the world," she wrote. She became an ardent supporter of suffrage, women's right to vote, as well as the efforts of the Socialist Party. Her views, like Macy's, became increasingly antiwar, anti–big business. She energetically promoted many different causes. If no one would publish her writing, she would publicly speak out against injustice. To do this, she knew she needed to improve her speaking voice and her appearance.

In 1909, she discovered a singing instructor, Charles A. White from Vermont, who helped her with voice lessons. White volunteered his expertise free of charge. Every Saturday he came to Wrentham and stayed until Sunday to give lessons. He learned the manual alphabet and directed her attention to her breathing so that she could learn how to achieve better control of the vowel and consonant sounds she made. What he discovered, much to Helen's disappointment, was that the methods used in her earlier training had actually made her voice worse. She would have to start all over again.

To improve her appearance, she had her damaged eyes surgically removed and replaced with glass ones in 1910. Her new eyes looked so realistic that no one realized they were not real. She could now be photographed face front and appeared more photogenic than ever.

As more and more of Annie's time and energy were spent coaching and working with Helen on her voice and her speeches, her marriage was

In 1909 Helen became a socialist and a suffragist. Four years later she published Out of the Dark, *a book of socialist writings.*

reaching the rupture point. It was, according to Macy, Annie's continual perfectionist nagging about Helen's voice that eventually helped drive him away. Macy, now drinking more than ever, moved out of Wrentham. Periodically he returned, but always left again after violent quarrels with Annie. Helen must have been aware of the terrible fights from the slamming doors and angry stomping. Annie, now quite heavy, was often ill. Her black moods began to consume her.

In May 1913 John left alone for Europe, where he would spend the next four months on an all-expense-paid holiday in Italy. Once again, it was Helen's lecture fees that footed his bill. After a tumultuous return and spending spree, he rented an apartment in Boston. In January 1914 he filed for divorce.

Helen and Annie in 1914

11.

On Stage

Between my experience and the experience of others there is no gulf of mute space which I may not bridge.
—Helen Keller, *The World I Live In*

HELEN VIEWED SPEECH as a "blessing" to herself and others. "It brings me into closer and tenderer relationship with those I love, and makes it possible for me to enjoy the sweet companionship of a great many persons from whom I should be entirely cut off if I could not talk." She admitted, however, that acquiring speech was not easy for an individual who could not hear and became doubly difficult for anyone who also lacked sight.

Yet Helen believed that speech was absolutely necessary for the deaf. "Without a language of some sort one is not a human being; without speech one is not a complete human being," Helen said. "Even when the speech is not beautiful there is a fountain of joy in uttering words. It is an emotional experience quite different from that which comes from spelled words."

For most Americans in the early part of the twentieth century, mutism—the inability to speak—was viewed as a tragic defect. Helen's view of herself as an "incomplete" human being was a reflection of this belief. Deaf education centered around achieving oral speech—at whatever cost. Even with financial resources, the best teachers, an extraordinary intellect, and persistence, Helen's goal remained elusive. But she refused to give up the dream that one day she would talk like other people.

After three years of hard work with White, Helen's voice suddenly became quite unmanageable. She discovered that wind, rain, or dust in the air affected the quality of her speech. If she was nervous, her "voice [was] sent on a rampage" and jumped low or high. She practiced morning and night. Sometimes she would succeed in speaking clearly, but she could not repeat the experience. She had no way of knowing how she sounded the first time.

Helen's voice was not beautiful. "The loneliest sound I have ever heard" is how Maude Howe Elliot, the daughter of former Perkins Institution director Samuel Gridley Howe, described Helen's voice: "Like waves breaking on the coast of some lonely desert island." When Helen spoke directly into the ear of hearing-impaired inventor Thomas Edison, he compared her voice to the unpleasant sound of steam exploding. Close friends who had grown accustomed to her speech said she reminded them of someone speaking with a heavy foreign accent. Only young children had little trouble understanding her, perhaps because they were less quick to judge and were used to "translating" one another's varied speech.

In spite of these difficulties, Helen was determined to use her voice to make her thoughts and opinions known. Boldly, she decided to go on the paid lecture circuit. She had no choice. Even with a yearly stipend from industrialist Andrew Carnegie and fees and royalties from writing books and magazine articles, she and Annie were once again nearly broke. "Our expenses were always a ravenous wolf devouring our finances," she wrote.

In February 1913, Helen made her first public speaking appearance in Montclair, New Jersey. She was terrified. The plan was that Annie, a good speaker, would begin the presentation with a short lecture about how she had taught Helen as a child. Then Helen would appear on the platform.

On her cue to enter, Helen felt as if she were going to her own hanging. "Terror invaded my flesh, my mind froze, my heart stopped beating. I kept repeating, 'What shall I do? What shall I do to calm this tumult within me?'"

Helen placed her fingers on Annie's mouth in order to show the audience how she could read lips. Annie gently pressed her arm to indicate when it was time for Helen to begin her speech, which Annie would repeat

The First Appearance on the Lecture Platform of

HELEN KELLER

And her Teacher Mrs. Macy (Anne M. Sullivan)

SUBJECT

"The Heart and the Hand," or the Right Use of our Senses

Under the exclusive Management of

J. B. POND LYCEUM BUREAU

Metropolitan Life Building

New York City

Helen and Annie went on the lecture circuit with this poster from 1913.

word for word to make sure that the audience understood. Helen froze, unable to say anything. "Words thronged to my lips, but no syllable could I utter. At last I forced a sound."

To Helen, her words boomed like a cannon going off. To someone in the audience, the sound she made was a mere whisper. She was too terrified to remember anything White had taught her during the past three years. "I felt my voice soaring and I knew that meant falsetto. Frantically, I dragged it down till my words fell about me like loose bricks."

When Helen finally finished—what seemed like many hours later to her—she rushed offstage and burst into tears. She felt like a complete failure.

Little did Helen realize that this would be the beginning of a fifty-year lecture career.

Each time Helen spoke, she tried to figure out what kinds of things her audiences wanted to hear. Like any good speaker, she adapted her talk to fit their interests and needs. She was especially interested in reaching

Helen's book, The World I Live In, *provided insights into the rich experiences of the deaf and blind. By 1912, Helen had published two books and countless articles.*

people who were poor, young, blind, deaf, or others she called "handicapped in the race of life." Her goal was always to give special encouragement. Sometimes she talked about happiness or the value of the senses. Most often she focused on "intimate dependence of human beings one upon another in the emergencies of life."

Throughout her life Helen tended to be critical of her speech and felt certain that audiences could hardly follow what she was trying to say. Sometimes she felt as if she swallowed the very words she wanted the audience to hear. "I pushed and strained. I pounded. I defeated myself with too much effort. I committed every sin against the dignity and grace of speech."

Speaking took incredible concentration on Helen's part. The slightest vibration or distraction could disorient her. "I almost collapsed when a chair was moved," she admitted, "or a streetcar rattled past the doors."

Yet Helen never gave up. She kept trying. She had a marvelous presence onstage. Audiences reacted to her radiant smile. She managed to create a kind of glow of warmth and enthusiasm even when deep down she wasn't feeling particularly happy. Her outfits were impeccably selected—the latest gowns and most fashionable hats. At age thirty, she looked youthful, stylish, and lovely—not at all the pathetic "defective" so many people thought of when they bothered to consider a deaf or blind person.

Audiences gave Helen something essential—a feeling of belonging, of being embraced. She no longer felt like an outsider. For someone so self-critical, she often expressed a sense of relief and gratitude when the audience's reaction was "very patient, whether they understood me or not, they showered me with good wishes and flowers and encouragement . . . little by little they began to get more of what I said."

Helen knew when an audience enjoyed a performance. She sensed the jarring movement of applause. Once, when a crowd seemed strangely silent, she feared they'd been too bored to clap. Later she discovered that they had been so engrossed in her teacher's story, they forgot to applaud. She felt this was the best compliment of all.

As their lecture circuit extended up and down the East Coast, Helen became more experienced in reading an audience's mood. "Before I say a word I feel its breath as it comes in little pulsations to my face. I sense its appreciation or indifference." She could tell from the thudding scrapes of heels and chairs if the crowd was impatient or bored, restless or agitated, friendly or hostile.

Lecture tours proved to be financial risks. Helen and Annie had to pay their own travel expenses. Often it was impossible to collect their share of money from the theater manager the night of their performance. Sometimes the theater manager did not show up. Sometimes he cheated them outright. Meanwhile, they had to pay their own manager his share, whether they were paid or not. If they complained or made a scene, the local papers would write unflattering articles about them.

As their travels took them farther and farther away from home, Helen sensed more keenly the enormous gap between the very rich and the very poor in America. During her visits as a teenager with Annie to some of the worst neighborhoods in New York City, Helen had experienced for the first time the stench of filth and the wretchedness of overcrowding and want of families crowded into tenement buildings. She read with avid interest Robert Hunter's *Poverty*, published in 1904, which estimated that there were at least ten million "underfed, underclothed, and poorly housed" in America. Of these, four million were public paupers who were dependent on public and private charity for survival. The rest had no such relief.

Meanwhile, every year more immigrants poured into the country, sky-rocketing from 448,572 in 1900 to 1,285,349 in 1907. Often these new-comers spoke little English and were desperate for any job—no matter how poorly paid or dangerous—to keep their families from starving to death.

Helen felt especially outraged about child labor abuses. In 1900 an estimated 1.7 million children between the ages of ten and fifteen worked in dangerous, smoky mills, factories, and mines where they earned less than a quarter a day. No federally enforced safety standards existed. "Scarce an hour passes without an accident," a European observer wrote in 1908 of a small steel town in Pennsylvania, "and no day without a fatal disaster. But what if *one* be crippled, if *one* life be extinguished among so many! Each place can be filled from *ten* men, all eager for it. . . . ."

Helen knew that for black Americans, the labor situation was even worse. From regular visits to her hometown she was aware that not much had changed in Alabama—or elsewhere—since she was a girl. Black workers were paid less, disenfranchised by the law so that they could not vote, and regularly humiliated. Every year during the first decade of the twentieth century, an estimated seventy blacks were lynched or burned at the stake. They faced segregated opportunities for second-rate housing and third-rate schools. Separate public rest rooms and restaurant entrances were marked "Colored." No existing labor union admitted blacks, so they formed their own.

Helen was an avid reader of newspaper coverage of the efforts to organize unions. Black or white, wherever labor unions were created, they often met with violent, bloody resistance. Newspapers focused on conflicts between strikers and "scabs"—workers who crossed the picket line to take up strikers' jobs. When strikes seriously disrupted business, management called in heavily armed militia. Some of the worst violence of the early twentieth century between strikers and militia took place on the slag-strewn hillsides of Ludlow Mine in Ludlow, Colorado, and outside the barbed wire fences of steel mills in Pennsylvania and New Jersey.

Helen wrote angry articles after she read of the thirteen men, women, and children killed during the "Ludlow Massacre" that took place in April 1914 on Colorado coal property belonging to John D. Rockefeller. "I have followed, step by step, the developments in Colorado, where women and children have been ruthlessly slaughtered," she told an interviewer at the time. "Mr. Rockefeller is the monster of capitalism. He gives charity and in the same breath he permits the helpless workmen, their wives and children to be shot down."

During the first decades of the twentieth century, millionaires like Rockefeller and others were building palatial homes and inviting guests to sumptuous twelve-course dinners that cost as much as $100,000. Meanwhile, the annual average salary of workers who worked six days a week, ten hours a day, amounted to only $400 to $500 per year. An unskilled laborer might make $460 in the North; in the South the same worker was lucky to be paid $300 a year, if he could find work. Women and children as young as ten were paid less than half that amount.

Helen was not afraid to ask hard, uncomfortable questions. "Why, in this land of great wealth, is there great poverty?" she demanded in an article published in 1912. "Why [do] children toil in the mills while thousands of men cannot get work, why [do] women who do nothing have thousands of dollars a year to spend?"

Helen was well aware of the latest developments in a long series of unsuccessful strikes. She had read the socialist works of German economist Karl Marx. Like so many Americans of her day, she could no longer view what was happening and remain unmoved. She wanted to do something practical and immediate.

From 1900 to 1912, a new reform movement was building in the United States as more and more people expressed a willingness to question what was happening around them. There was a basic feeling that "citizens needed to look out for the interests of all the people," historian Frederick Lewis Allen explained, "not simply a privileged few." Campaigns were mounted for all kinds of reforms—everything from ending hookworm to ridding local government of corruption.

People rich and poor backed different programs. Some rallied behind a push to improve factory working conditions, others marched to Congress to create pure food and drug laws. Women in many states struggled to convince their states to allow them to vote. Meanwhile, expanded newspaper and magazine circulation helped to promote the first investigative reporting of government and the economy.

"Many young women full of devotion and goodwill have been engaged in superficial charities," Helen complained in 1912. "They have tried to feed the hungry without knowing the causes of poverty. They have tried to minister to the sick without understanding the cause of disease. They have tried to raise up fallen sisters without knowing the brutal arm of necessity that struck them down. . . . We attempt social reforms where we need social transformations. We mend small things and leave the great things untouched."

Helen did not believe that real change was happening fast enough. In 1909 she had quietly joined the Socialist Party in Massachusetts. This was considered a radical labor movement that offered women and men a philosophy and worldview to explain their present-day problems and give them a vision of a better future. Socialists believed that industry management must be in the hands of the workers. Government had to change as well. Capitalism and free enterprise were viewed as the enemy.

Eugene V. Debs, who became a presidential candidate of the Socialist Party, was a friend of Helen's later in life. Debs described capitalists, or the owners of the factories and mills, as the people who spent their time gambling, drinking champagne, choosing judges, buying editors, hiring preachers, preaching morals, bequeathing the earth to their descendants while "the other side does the work, early and late, in heat and cold; they sweat and groan and bleed and die." In 1900, Eugene V. Debs ran for president and won 96,000 votes. By 1912, he had nearly 901,000 votes.

To most middle-class Americans and owners of businesses, socialism was considered "a grim and leveling monster." Newspaper reports made it hard to distinguish between socialists and anarchists, a movement that called for violent overthrow of all governments. Socialism "had simply come to mean unruly mobs led by frowsy wives carrying torches soaked with kerosene," historian Ben Maddow explained. Helen embraced socialism with a passion. Like many women at the time, her involvement was one of her first self-confident experiences in group solidarity and group action.

As the First World War raged in Europe and America teetered toward involvement, Helen was invited to take part in a demonstration with the Women's Peace Party. More than fifteen hundred women dressed all in black or in white with black armbands marched silently down Fifth Avenue in New York City on August 29, 1914, to call for peace in Europe. Large crowds watched respectfully. That evening, Helen made an impassioned speech for pacifism and socialism in crowded Carnegie Hall.

"The future of the world rests in the hands of America," she announced. "The future of America rests on the leaders of 80 million working men and women and their children." To end the war and capitalism "all you need to do . . . is to straighten up and fold your arms."

These were thrilling, dangerous words. Newspapers did not quite know what to make of Helen the socialist. Wasn't she being unpatriotic? They accused Annie Sullivan Macy of brainwashing Helen, even though Annie was neither a socialist nor a suffragist and was often shocked by Helen's statements.

For Helen, her connection with audiences during these impassioned speeches was profoundly moving. "I can hardly realize that those hundreds upon hundreds of people whose presence I still feel came to hear me," she later wrote. "But they did, and I have never again felt separated from my fellow men by the silent dark! Any sense of isolation is impossible since the doors of my heart were thrown open, and all the world came in."

Helen saw the political and economic situation as a kind of contest between Good and Evil. There was no room for shadings of gray. Her sense of commitment and mission to the working class was real. As an outsider herself, she identified with the outcast, the downtrodden, the underprivileged. And she understood how the fate of the disabled resembled that of the other oppressed minorities—whether they were underpaid, abused workers or disenfranchised blacks. The cause of suffering of both was the same: an economic system that enslaved them.

"My family all belonged to the master class, and were proud of their birth and social prestige, and they held slaves," she wrote in a revealing letter to the *Brooklyn Eagle* in 1912. "Now, even since childhood, my feelings have been with their slaves. I am dispossessed with them. I am disenfranchised with them, I feel all the bitterness of their humiliation when a white man may take a job or a home he wants, while they are driven out of houses and churches—nay, and are even terrorized and lynched if they compete in doing profitable work for the master class. And my sympathies are with all the workers who struggle for justice. . . . "

In 1913 she again shocked her mother and the rest of her family in

Alabama by publishing *Out of the Dark*, a book containing many essays including "How I Became a Socialist." Her public had a hard time believing that beloved Helen Keller could have created such a book of her own free will.

Helen embraced movements against child labor. She spoke out in favor of votes for women and supported an amendment to the Constitution that would give women suffrage. This amendment had been introduced in 1869 but had not gained enough momentum for passage. She spoke out in favor of birth control, which was considered an immoral practice, and was condemned by churchmen and deplored by civic leaders. Public advocates of birth control like Margaret Sanger, who sent her book, *Family Limitation*, through the mail in 1912, had to flee the country to avoid a federal indictment.

Helen saw a connection between the restriction of information about birth control, big business, child labor, and low wages. In 1915 she declared openly in the New York socialist newspaper *The Call* that factory owners "for the sake of profits alone, deliberately encourage the workers to have large families, that their little ones may be driven to labor" for minimal pay.

Meanwhile, in Helen's own household important economic changes were taking place. With the departure of John Macy in 1914, Scottish-born Polly Thomson had joined the staff as secretary-housekeeper. Five years younger than Helen, Polly was a willing, loyal worker. Although she supported Helen's political views, she had her own secret cravings that would have appalled most socialists. There was nothing Polly enjoyed more than expensive hats, jewelry, and furs.

In 1914 Helen faced new economic and personal crises.

12.
Love and Exile

I look upon the whole world as my fatherland, and every war has to me a horror of family feud.
—Helen's Speech at Labor Forum,
New York City, December 19, 1915

$\mathscr{I}$N THE FALL OF 1916, Helen returned to Wrentham discouraged and worried about the future. Her lecture tour during the previous summer had been a failure. No one wanted to hear about peace. No one wanted to think about reforms like women's suffrage or child labor laws. "They had come to hear me talk about happiness and perhaps recite, 'Nearer My God to Thee,'" Helen wrote. "They didn't want to have peace of mind disturbed by talk of war, especially when so many didn't think it would actually ever happen."

Helen believed otherwise. She read with grim foreboding the front-page coverage of the war in Europe 3,000 miles away across the Atlantic. A growing number of Americans were convinced that it was only a matter of time before the United States joined the fight.

For the past two years Germany and Austria-Hungry had faced off in a stalemate against the allied powers of France, England, Italy, and Russia. The Great War, later known as World War One, used deadly new technology: submarines, quick-firing artillery, flame throwers, chemical warfare, and military aircraft. Soldiers often fought from trenches protected by barbed wire in "no-man's-zones," strafed of trees, houses, and any sign of life. It was modern war, total war, that in two years, from 1914 to 1916, claimed four million casualties—including one million deaths—as the fighting leapfrogged to Africa, Asia, the Middle East, and across the Atlantic, Pacific, and Indian Oceans.

While America stumbled toward formal declaration of war against Germany, President Woodrow Wilson began a national campaign to whip up patriotism and pro-war sentiment. Congress set up programs for national security and announced plans to double the size of the army. The Council of National Defense was created to coordinate industry and resources.

Helen found these trends deeply disturbing. Like other socialists, she believed that war brought wealth and power to the ruling class and suffering and death to the workers, while producing a sinister spirit of "passion, unreason, race hatred and false patriotism."

Even more alarming to Helen was Annie's deteriorating health. Deeply depressed since the end of her marriage, overweight Annie wore black and wept constantly. She developed a bad cough that was diagnosed as possible tuberculosis, a then fatal disease that destroys the lungs. Doctors ordered her to take a "rest cure" in Saranac, a spa near Lake Placid in upstate New York. She would be accompanied by Polly Thomson, who had quietly become an essential member of the household. Meanwhile, Helen would travel with her mother to Montgomery, Alabama, where her sister lived with her husband, Warren Tyson. The couple had three daughters, Katherine, Patty, and Mildred.

Exile did not please thirty-six-year-old Helen, who felt very alone and anxious about her own future. What if Annie died? How would she be able to continue her work? "My experience of the summer had brought home to me the fact that few people were interested in my aims and aspirations," Helen later wrote. "Once more I was overwhelmed by a sense of my isolation."

One evening before her departure to Alabama, Helen sat in her study at Wrentham preoccupied with her troubles. Her secretary, twenty-nine-year-old Peter Fagan, who had been hired as Polly's replacement, came

*Annie's health began to fail in 1916. While she went to Puerto Rico with Polly
to recover, Helen became engaged to be married.*

into the room and sat beside her. He knew the manual alphabet and Braille. Fagan was a radical socialist and a former assistant of John Macy. "For a long time he held my hand in silence," Helen remembered, "then he began talking to me tenderly. I was surprised that he cared so much about me. There was sweet comfort in his loving words. I listened all a-tremble."

Fagan proposed marriage. He promised to "always be near to help me in the difficulties of life . . . and do as much as he could of the work my teacher had done for me," Helen wrote. The idea both stunned and pleased her. But knowing her conservative mother's disapproval of Fagan's extreme political views, she agreed with him that it would be better to keep their marriage plans a secret for a while. Meanwhile, Fagan slipped away to Boston and applied for a marriage license.

The *Boston Globe* broke the story before Helen could explain anything to her mother. "What have you been doing with that creature?" her mother demanded as she suddenly burst into her bedroom. "The papers are full of a dreadful story about you and him. What does it all mean? Tell me!"

Even though Helen was a grown woman and a worldwide celebrity, she did not feel confident enough to declare her intentions to her mother. Terrified, she denied everything. She even lied to Annie, who was bedridden and about to leave for the Lake Placid spa. Helen's rationale, she later wrote, was that the shock might be too much for her teacher. Her denial proved to be an easy lie. Annie thought Fagan too "insignificant" and unattractive to pose a real threat as a suitor.

Helen's mother thought otherwise. Immediately, she ordered Fagan out of the house. She demanded that Helen issue a statement of denial to the press through their lawyer. Helen did so, all the while secretly planning an elopement. Communicating through Braille notes, she and Fagan planned to stage an abduction. It was an odd, romantic scheme. While Helen was traveling with her mother by boat to Savannah, Fagan would kidnap her and they would steal away on a train to Florida, where they would be married.

At the last moment, Helen's mother found out about the elopement and changed their plans. In November 1916, she and her daughter took the train to Alabama. Fagan sailed alone.

Stubbornly, he showed up several more times once Helen and her mother reached Montgomery. On one occasion he was spied on Mildred's porch spelling rapidly into Helen's hand. Mildred's husband rushed to get his gun to scare him away.

One night, some time later, Helen was discovered on the porch waiting with her bag packed. Fagan never came. "Or if he did, he realized before he got very close that there was trouble afoot and there was no use getting mixed up in it," wrote Nella Braddy Henney, an editor and friend of Helen's who interviewed her about the episode many years later.

Fagan faded from the scene and so did Helen's hopes of marriage. "The brief love," she wrote, "will remain in my life, a little island of joy surrounded by dark waters. I am glad that I have had the experience

Helen in 1913

of being loved and desired. The fault was not in the loving, but in the circumstances."

Like so many people at the time, Helen's mother believed that the disabled should not be allowed to marry. This view reflected her traditional, overprotective southern upbringing and something of her own ambivalent feelings about female sexuality.

As for Annie's opinion about Helen marrying, she left no record. During the high points of Helen's romantic drama in December 1917, Annie and Polly had impetuously decided to leave dreary Lake Placid for an expensive trip by ship to San Juan, Puerto Rico. While sunning herself on the beach, Annie got the idea to order their chauffeur and car shipped to the island, an extravagance they could not afford.

It's doubtful that Annie would have supported Helen's marriage plan had she known about it. Helen's marriage would have changed everything about the relationship between Annie and Helen. Annie depended on Helen not only for her identity as "miracle worker," but for complete financial support as well.

Helen spent the next five months in Alabama with her family, who did not know quite what to make of her anymore. She tried to fit into the rounds of constant visiting and what she described as endless boring discussions of "parties, dresses, babies, weddings, and obesity."

The most exciting moment in her visit came when she smelled smoke one night after she had gone to bed. Helen's keen sense of smell helped save herself, her mother, and her sister's family. "I smelt tar and burning wood," she wrote in a letter to Annie in February 1917. "I sprang up, threw a window open and rushed to mother's room. She found a flame six feet high in my room. . . . " A faulty flue caused the fire to start directly under Helen's bed. Fortunately, everyone safely evacuated the house.

After this initial turmoil, Helen managed to adjust to the slow-moving pace of Montgomery. However, she could never get used to tempering her radical political opinions. She openly supported the Industrial Workers of the World, a militant labor organization that advocated sabotage and other forms of violence if necessary.

Southern criticism of Helen quickly spread when the editor of an Alabama newspaper found out that she had dared to donate money to the National Association for the Advancement of Colored People (NAACP). Always against segregation, Helen had written a letter stating, "The outrages against the colored people are a denial of Christ. The central fire of his teaching is equality." This letter was reprinted in the NAACP journal. Her mother and the rest of her family were horrified when the *Selma Journal* accused Helen of being a traitor to fellow white southerners and of being an individual whose mind had been "thoroughly poisoned" by a Yankee teacher.

On April 6, 1917, President Woodrow Wilson signed the war resolution Congress had passed after hearing his famous speech. Wilson had argued that the United States needed to become involved in the war in Europe to "keep the world safe for democracy." Three days later Helen despondently wrote to Annie, "There is little to tell—little that is bright or good. All happiness has left us with the departure of peace from our land."

The country feverishly geared up for war. Factories churned out more armaments. Bands played patriotic tunes in front of draft boards across the country as 24 million men registered for the draft. George M. Cohan's catchy hit song "Over There" echoed on the streets:

Over there, over there
Send the word, send the word, over there
That the Yanks are coming, the Yanks are coming,
The drums rum-tumming everywhere.

With the country now officially at war, Annie and Polly had to leave their island paradise. They booked the first boat back to the United States, where they were joyfully reunited with Helen.

Helen's life would never be the same, however. Wrentham, her home for nearly thirteen years, had to be sold in 1917. She no longer had enough money to pay for the upkeep of the rambling house and numerous acres. Parting with the house that contained so many sad and happy memories must have been difficult. "I shall always think of it as home," Helen wrote.

Tanned and rested, fifty-year-old Annie, who always enjoyed the attention and relaxation that retreat into illness provided, immediately began to complain of new aches and pains. She could not sleep. She could not read. Helen once again hurried to her rescue and rented a cabin in Vermont for her teacher's continuing recovery. While Annie was reexamined by doctors at Lake Placid at the end of the summer, Helen boldly hiked up Whiteface Mountain with Polly. When they returned, they were delighted by the wonderful news. Annie was fine.

Happily, Helen, Annie, and Polly found another house in Forest Hills, just fourteen miles from the center of New York City. They moved in in October 1917 with all their belongings, including their Great Dane, Sieglinde. At first this seemed like a fresh start for Helen. She felt encouraged by sketchy news arriving about the "proletariat revolution in Russia" and the fall of the tsar. No one at the time knew how many lives had been lost in the bloody overthrow or what had become of the tsar or his family. Meanwhile, Helen spoke before the Intercollegiate Socialist Society at New York University about the "new day for all mankind."

There were, however, clouds of darkness on the horizon. The government had begun a crackdown on all political dissidents. Leading socialists such as Eugene V. Debs and Rose Pastor Stokes were locked up in jail for saying that citizens should not support the war, claiming the conflict was "for the profiteers." Helen's friend, anarchist Emma Goldman, was arrested for trying to sabotage the Draft Act. Using new wartime powers, government officials shut down or censored socialist and other antiwar newspapers.

Violent strikes and racial conflict erupted in different locations throughout the country because of unequal treatment of laborers. International Workers of the World leader "Big" Bill Haywood and 112 other men were rounded up by agents of the Department of Justice in September 1917 and sent to prison for inciting strikes. Haywood was eventually sentenced to twenty years.

After presenting a carefully worded speech to a group of soldiers, Helen openly invited newspapermen to her new home so that she could discuss what she called "the harshness, intolerance, and mad folly of those who are persecuting, imprisoning and lynching Socialists, 'I.W.W.s' and other 'agitators.'" Only one reporter showed up and did not write down anything Helen said.

Amazingly, in the midst of the political repression and hysteria and as her comrades were being muzzled or destroyed for their political opinions, Helen remained unscathed. In spite of her extreme views, she had become a kind of icon to the public. No one could believe she had radical views. No one could believe she would say anything that wasn't positive and joyful. She had become an authentic American heroine who had risen above seemingly impossible adversity. That was all anyone cared to believe.

Unfortunately, being an authentic American heroine did not pay mounting bills. Not only did Helen have to support ailing Annie, she had to foot the costs of Polly the spendthrift, a maid, a growing herd of dogs (at one point she owned seven), a chauffeur, and a cook. Extravagant gifts to friends and Polly's shopping sprees on Fifth Avenue took their toll on Helen's finances. Once again, she was broke.

Boldly, Helen seized upon the one available moneymaking scheme open to her at the time. She went to Hollywood to accept an offer to star in a motion picture about her life.

Helen was called "Eighth Wonder of the World" in the Deliverance
poster celebrating the film's opening.

13.
Bright Lights of Hollywood and Vaudeville

I lost all sense of permanence, and even now I never feel really as if I am living at home.

—Helen Keller, *Midstream*

$\mathcal{W}$HEN HELEN, ANNIE, AND POLLY ARRIVED in California in the spring of 1918 to film *Deliverance*, the uplifting story of Helen's life, Hollywood was just a slapdash little town on the edge of the desert. It was a place where anything might occur—cavalry charges, houses bursting into flames, or cars hurling off cliffs. Hollywood was quickly becoming the production center for the silent film industry. These enormously popular, state-of-the-art movies had no soundtrack but plenty of action. Actors and actresses dressed up in wigs and bright white makeup and gestured dramatically. Their accompanying written dialogue appeared on screen after their scenes.

Helen found Hollywood fascinating. One time while she was out on a horseback ride in the desert, she was surprised to discover a lone rider dressed in a complete Indian outfit. Her companion called to him so that Helen could meet a "real western Indian" in person. Helen politely asked if she might touch his feathered headdress.

"Sure," the Indian replied in perfect English. "The lady can feel me as much as she likes."

It turned out that he was not an authentic warrior. He was simply an actor waiting for a camera crew.

Surprises were always happening to Helen in Hollywood. She delighted in so much unexpected excitement. Annie did not. Helen enjoyed meeting celebrity performer Charlie Chaplin and the most famous acting couple of the day, Mary Pickford and Douglas Fairbanks. Annie felt snubbed when Helen was invited to glamorous parties and she wasn't.

Helen soon realized that filming the story of her life was going to be anything but glamorous. Work began in early June for the film posters described as "the Photo-Play Beautiful" of Helen Keller, "the Eighth Wonder of the World." Early scenes in Helen's life were played by a winsome child actress who posed beside the pump as her "teacher" pumped water into her hand, and another attractive ingenue played the "college" version of Helen. Helen performed herself in later life. In these scenes Helen wore a scratchy blond wig, stifling costumes, and thick white makeup as she struggled to stand for hours without withering in front of intensely hot mercury-vapor lights.

*Polly, Helen, and Annie visited on the Hollywood set
with film star Charlie Chaplin.*

Helen, her brother Phillips, and her mother appeared
in the film Deliverance *in 1918.*

Communication was a problem on the set. Helen felt especially awkward whenever someone insisted that she "act natural." She had no idea what "act natural" looked like. The director tapped the floor with his foot to send her signals for her cues: when to dance, pour tea for a caller, or comb her hair. The script even called for her to demonstrate how a deaf and blind person got into bed and slept with her eyes shut. Most of her time, however, was spent waiting for her next scene.

"There I sat or stood for a picture, growing hotter and hotter, my hands more and more moist as light poured upon me," Helen recalled. "My embarrassment caused my brow and nose to shine inartistically."

But she did not give up even when it soon became clear that major and somewhat bizarre changes would be made in the script. The screenwriter declared Helen's life "too boring." The director staged a fight between "Knowledge and Ignorance" outside the "Cave of Time" for the "spirit of infant Helen." Elaborate, absurd dream scenes were introduced with casts of hundreds on a scorched hillside that was supposed to look like

Jerusalem. Helen was even given a mythical lover, Ulysses, who suffered in a cruel shipwreck scene wearing a wild curly beard.

Another change in the script called for Helen to pose as Joan of Arc. She had to ride on a restless white horse while holding a nasty-tasting trumpet to her mouth. In another new scene she demonstrated that she was brave enough to fly in the open cockpit of an airplane. Unlike her stint as Saint Joan, she enjoyed flying enormously. "I have never had such a satisfying sense of physical liberty," she wrote.

The film cost an enormous sum to produce for the time—more than $250,000. When *Deliverance* was finally released in August 1919 in New York City, Helen did not attend the opening. An Actors' Equity strike was in progress and she refused to cross the picket line. Although reviews were enthusiastic, the film was a complete economic flop. The producers lost their investment and neither Helen nor Annie made any of the money they had been promised. Helen, Annie, and Polly had to borrow cash to travel from California back to Forest Hills.

Part of the lack of interest in the film had to do with the changing times. The war officially ended June 28, 1919, when the Peace of Paris was signed. Germany was defeated. More than 75,000 Americans had been killed in battle, were wounded, or had died from disease during nineteen months of fighting. When the nearly four million surviving soldiers returned home, many discovered that their jobs were gone and that prices for food, clothing, and housing had skyrocketed. People wanted light, comic entertainment—not a film that was serious and idealistic.

Society had changed since the war. Women who drove ambulances, manned hospitals, and worked in armament factories and clerical jobs during the war were no longer content being second-class citizens. One of the few postwar bright spots was the passage by Congress in June 1919 of the Nineteenth Amendment guaranteeing women the right to vote.

Like many Americans, Helen sensed that the war had been a kind of watershed. Nothing would ever be the same again. The year 1919 was marked by mounting labor unrest, violent strikes, and bloody racial clashes. That year alone twenty-five race riots broke out all over the country. Thirteen days of rioting in Chicago left fifteen whites and twenty-three blacks dead. A mob of twenty thousand in Omaha burned a courthouse and lynched a black man.

Hatred once directed against the German kaiser was now directed toward "reds"—socialists and Bolsheviks. It was a dangerous time to speak out on the hypocrisy of having won a war to end all wars when, in the United States, Helen said, "Negroes may be massacred and their property burned." In spite of stepped-up threats against "Communist agitators," she did not mince words a year later, on December 31, 1920, at New York's Madison Square Garden, when she hailed the creation of the Soviet Republic of Russia, declaring "Onward, Comrades, all together, onward to the bright redeeming dawn!"

Meanwhile, Helen had to find a practical way to survive. She was broke. In 1919 help came in an unexpected offer. Would she consider auditioning for the highly popular vaudeville circuit, a variety show of dancers, singers, acrobats, comedians, magicians, and performing animals? Annie was appalled by such an undignified idea.

But Helen was not. The pay was excellent. They did not have to do as much traveling as they had on the lecture circuit. They could stay in one theater for a week. "I found the world of vaudeville much more amusing than the world I had always lived in, and I liked it," wrote Helen. She delighted in "the rush, glare, and noise of the theater" and enjoyed the company of the other actors and actresses.

She especially enjoyed the audiences. "I liked to feel the warm tide of human life pulsing round and round me." The crowds responded enthusiastically to Helen's performance as well. For twenty minutes during a matinee and twenty minutes during the evening, she and Annie performed their act almost daily from 1919 until 1922. Dressed in fancy evening gowns, they came onstage to a drawing room setting complete with crackling fire in the fireplace. Helen had her own theme song, "The Star of Happiness," played by the orchestra.

At their standing-room-only opening in February 1919, fifty-three-year-old Annie described in her ringing, clear voice how she had taught

Helen backstage putting on her makeup before a vaudeville show in 1920

Helen the meaning of language. Then Helen demonstrated how she lip-read and learned to speak her first phrase, "I am not dumb now." Annie repeated everything radiant Helen said to make sure she was understood. At the end, they took questions from the audience. Annie finger-spelled the questions and Helen gave prepared, often humorous answers orally, with help again from Annie:

Does talking tire you?
Did you ever hear of a woman who tired of talking?

Do you close your eyes when you sleep?
I guess I do, but I never stayed awake to see.

Sometimes the questions were more serious:

What do you think of the Ku Klux Klan?
I like them about as much as I do a hornet's nest.
Who is your favorite hero in real life?
Eugene V. Debs. He dared to do what other men were afraid to do.

Helen and Annie traveled so constantly across the country by train and car, that Helen soon felt as if she had no home. Although she enjoyed meeting new people and having new experiences, she admitted that it was wearying to live in a hotel where she couldn't leave or move about without someone accompanying her. "At such times I am painfully aware of the lack of personal liberty, which, next to idleness, is the hardest part of being blind."

While in Los Angeles in 1921, Helen heard the news that her mother had died. She went on with their act in the show, she later wrote, even though "every fiber of my being cried out at the thought of facing the audience, but it had to be done." Once again, Helen's deep religious views helped her get through this difficult time.

That same year, while performing in Toronto, Annie became too ill to go on stage. Steadily growing blind and always uncomfortable with the garish, bright lights and what she felt was the uncouth company of parrots, monkeys, and tap-dancers, Annie gradually withdrew from the act. Her place was taken by the quiet Polly, who, with her pleasant Scottish accent, surprised everyone by rising to the occasion like a real trouper. By 1922, Polly had taken over Annie's stage role completely. From that point on, Annie stayed backstage when she traveled with Helen and Polly on tour or remained at home in Forest Hills with her dogs and books.

In 1932 Helen, Annie, and Polly posed with two of their many dogs.

14.
A New Career

We differ, blind and seeing, one from another, not in our senses, but in the use we make of them, in the imagination and courage with which we seek wisdom beyond our senses.

—Helen Keller, *The World I Live In*

WHEN CROWDS NO LONGER JAMMED THE THEATER to see their act, Helen's involvement with the vaudeville circuit eventually ended. Now forty-three, with aging, semi-blind Annie in tow, Helen was once again searching for a way to support herself and her household.

In late 1923 she found a whole new avenue for her talents and energy when she was unexpectedly tapped by the American Foundation for the Blind, a national clearinghouse of information, books, and education for the blind founded that year. Based in New York, the foundation was headed by a forceful director, Robert Irwin, who was blinded at age five and had gone on to become the University of Washington's first blind graduate.

Irwin decided that Helen was the perfect person to spearhead a campaign to raise money for an endowment to keep the new organization running. Helen Keller's name, Irwin knew, was instantly recognized. She was attractive, intelligent, full of energy and hope—the perfect symbol.

During their first seven gatherings in New Jersey, Helen and Annie spoke before ten thousand people and collected nearly $8,000 for the foundation. "The plan is for Teacher and me," Helen wrote to her sister, "to go from city to city, hold meetings and solicit funds. We understand that most of the meetings will take place afternoons in the private houses of society people."

Helen and Annie's expenses would be covered. They would be on the road again. The problem was whether Annie, whose health was failing, would be able to hold up under the pressure. She had strange mood swings that often pitted her against the foundation board, which had finally agreed to provide them with a salary of $2,000 a month. The ambitious goal was to raise two million dollars for the foundation's endowment fund.

What remained unspoken was that Helen was not to pepper fund-raising talks with any of her radical political ideas. She managed, however, in 1924 to write a rousing letter supporting Robert La Follette, an early pacifist against U.S. entrance into the war who was running for president as a third-party candidate from Wisconsin. "So long as I confine my activities to social service and the blind, they compliment me extravagantly, calling me 'archpriestess of the sightless,' 'wonder woman,' and 'a modern miracle,'" Helen complained privately in a letter to La Follette. "But when it comes to a discussion of poverty, and I maintain that it is the result of wrong economics—that the industrial system under which we live is at the root of much of the physical deafness and blindness in the world—that is a different matter!"

The foundation was not pleased to find out she was pro–La Follette. But the grueling campaign began on schedule. From 1924 until 1927, Helen traveled coast to coast and addressed 250,000 people at 249 meetings in 123 cities. She gave countless interviews to newspapers and magazines and attended innumerable luncheons and receptions. She kept her word to the foundation and did not venture publicly into politics again for another twenty years, until 1944, when she endorsed Franklin D. Roosevelt for a fourth term.

Helen's passion as a tireless reformer and crusader served the foundation well. Helen crisscrossed the United States and made several trips to Europe to raise funds, making as many as five speeches a day, while also visiting countless schools for the deaf and blind. She wrote innumerable letters of thanks and corresponded with donors from all over the world. In 1931, she participated in the first World Council for the Blind with representatives from thirty-two nations. Helen appeared before Congress to help push through the Pratt-Smoots Bill, which provided funding for a national system of public libraries for the blind.

She took time off from fund-raising to write *My Religion*, published in 1927, and another autobiography, *Midstream: My Later Life*, which came out in 1929. She worked with Nella Braddy Henney, a friend and editor, who recorded in her journal her first day working with Helen in January 1927: "I went very slowly, though as fast as I could and how she was able to keep up with me was more than I know, for by the time I was spelling the end of a sentence I had forgotten what the beginning was, but she seemed to have no trouble."

Heaps of paper covered the floor. Helen had her own system to keep track of where she was in writing the book. She used a hairpin to prick an appropriate phrase from the typewritten page. "Hammering out ideas without being able to see what one is doing is one of the most exasperating trials of blindness," Helen wrote.

Once a chapter was edited, Nella read the new copy to Annie, who translated the pages into the manual alphabet for Helen. "I am not an easy, prolific writer. . . . When I remember the books I have written," Helen later wrote, "it is with pain, not joy; for I cannot forget the stern labor that went into them."

Annie's failing health was reaching a crisis point. She was almost completely blind, frail, and senile. Unlike Helen, who viewed her blindness and deafness as opportunities for courage, Annie's loss of sight came late in life and filled her with bitter desperation and hopelessness. Unlike Helen, Annie had no faith in religion. She viewed old age as a pointless struggle.

Helen and Annie reversed roles. Helen became her teacher's guide. She worked hard to keep Annie from despair. In 1930 she thought a trip to Ireland would help. But a visit to her parents' homeland only made Annie more melancholy. "When one stops talking in Ireland," Annie complained of the desolate bog-lands and rocky wastes, "one hears the murmur of grieving and death. One feels that death and the sweet-breathing earth are one." To Annie, London was nothing but "a vast crouching beast."

Helen and Annie returned to New York in the midst of the Great Depression. Millions of people across the country were still out of work after the stock market crash of 1929. By 1932 about twelve million were unemployed—nearly one out of every four workers. Banks closed their doors. Mines and factories stopped operation. Mortgages were foreclosed and farm families were evicted. At the foundation, there was little cash to spare. Helen was busy writing books and did not go back on the road for the foundation until 1932. Because of the deepening depression, the eighty meetings Helen and Polly attended and spoke before resulted in only $20,000.

Fortunately throughout this time, generous "Major" Moses Charles Migel, the foundation's executive director and a retired silk manufacturer, provided personal financial help above and beyond Helen's regular salary. Although he had a prickly relationship with Annie, his private funds helped take care of her mounting medical bills and vacations.

Helen heeded Migel's advice and took nervous, discouraged Annie to the Catskill Mountains north of New York City. In October 1935, she organized a trip to Jamaica, hoping that the tropical island might remind Annie of her beloved Puerto Rico. Finally, in August of 1936, Helen rented an oceanside cottage in Greenport, Long Island. "That was our desperate last effort to strengthen her so that her life might be tolerable," Helen remembered. Annie surprised Helen one day by walking out into the waves. She became dizzy and collapsed. Helen and Polly had to half-carry her back inside. After being hospitalized, Annie returned to Forest Hills.

Helen's last memory of her teacher of fifty years was an October evening when Annie was fully awake, sitting in an armchair. Polly, Helen, and a neighbor named Herbert Haas gathered around her. "She was laughing while Herbert told her about the rodeo he had just seen," Helen recalled. "She spelled to me all he said, and how tenderly she fondled my hand! . . . Afterwards she drifted into a coma from which she never awoke on earth." When seventy-year-old Annie died on October 20, 1936, fifty-six-year-old Helen was sitting beside her bed, holding her hand.

Annie's ashes were placed in a special memorial at the National

On a trip to Japan Helen and Polly wore kimonos and admired an exotic bird with a long tail.

Cathedral in Washington, D.C. She was the first woman to be honored for achievements in this way. A few days later, Helen and Polly left for Scotland by ship. Many close friends of Helen wondered what would become of her now that Annie was gone. Some suggested that she should move back to the South, live with her sister in comfortable seclusion, and give up public life.

Helen had no intention of giving up. "Life is a daring adventure or nothing," she wrote in a diary she kept on her first trip away from the United States after Annie's death. Writing helped her deal with her own grief. It also helped her express her own need to "stand on my own feet socially and economically." She was determined to "shape my life anew and confirm further my message to the handicapped." She wanted to prove that she was an independent person apart from Annie Sullivan Macy.

When Helen and Polly returned, they sold the house at Forest Hills and moved to Westport, Connecticut. They named their new home Arcan Ridge. In 1937, Helen and Polly traveled to Japan where Helen gave ninety-seven lectures to enormous throngs of cheering people in thirty-nine cities to raise money—an incredible 35 million yen—for the blind and deaf Japanese. "No foreign visitor had ever been accorded such an enthusiastic reception," wrote Nicholas C. Rhoen and Jami Hooper in an article for the *Akita Journal.*

As Helen traveled in Japan and Europe, she was aware of a new rising tide of militarism and buildup of another enormous war machine. On her trip throughout Europe, she wrote with alarm in her journal in 1936: "To the world, black clouds threatening Europe's peace hopes, wicked anti-Semitic persecution and the sickening barbarities in Madrid." Only three years earlier, on May 10, 1933, her books had been among those burned by Nazis in a huge bonfire attended by thousands of Berlin onlookers.

Helen's insights would prove prophetic. By September 1, 1939, the world would once again be plunged into war—this one more terrible than the first with a total of nearly fifteen million battle deaths and an estimated total cost of one trillion dollars. Fighting would occur in Europe, Africa, and Asia and involve troops from countries all over the world.

Helen, always eager to ease the fear of the newly disabled, made seventy trips to American army and navy hospitals in 1944 to visit blind soldiers. "You are the most impressive and stimulating visitor we have had at our hospital," one staff member wrote to her, "and that puts you ahead of the Hollywood blondes, brunettes, and playboys."

From 1943 until 1955, Helen traveled tirelessly to hospitals to visit the blind, deaf, and wounded soldiers. On one trip to the Naval Hospital in

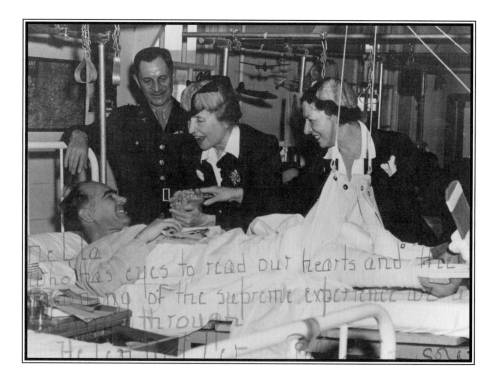

Helen and Polly visited wounded soldiers during World War I and II. The letter to her friend Nella Braddy Henney reads: "Who has eyes to read our hearts and the meaning of the supreme experience we are going through?"

Philadelphia, she was accompanied by her neighbors, sculptor Jo Davidson and his wife.

"Here were depressed and sullen young men, feeling the injustice of it all," Davidson remembered. "Helen's presence in their midst was something very moving to see. She spoke to them of overcoming their handicaps as if it were almost a privilege. One of the boys was learning to use a typewriter. Helen typed out a message on it and read it to the boys in the ward. Their faces lit up. One felt that Helen had left behind that priceless thing—hope."

During two world wars Helen had witnessed enormous human suffering. For her, the critical turning point in her antiwar resolve came in 1948. That year she and Polly visited the "black, silent hole" that had once been Hiroshima and Nagasaki, the Japanese cities leveled by the atomic bombs dropped in 1945 by the United States and its allies. Helen toured the smoky, ash-strewn rubble, spoke with survivors, and felt the scarred faces of radiation victims. This experience, she later wrote, "scorched a deep scar" in her soul. She felt more determined than ever to work for peace.

Helen on a tour of South Africa in 1950 met with a father and his son, who glanced anxiously at the camera.

In the next thirteen years, Helen traveled to thirty-five different countries on five continents to make presentations and raise money on behalf of the disabled. This involved countless hours of composing, memorizing, and practicing speeches. And throughout her later vagabond years, she was piloted by Polly, who had no sense of humor and was often rather insecure. While Polly was not as imaginative, well-read, or amusing as Annie, she was a tireless worker and a sturdy, indomitable traveler.

Polly's photographs make her seem rather mousy, with undistinguished brown hair and eyes. "Her face," one friend said in the 1920s, "was a mask for her thoughts and feelings." She had excellent taste, although with a pronounced attraction for expensive jewelry, designer hats, and fur coats. She kept Helen looking fashionable and attractive in all her appearances.

Born in Glasgow, Scotland, of middle-class parents, Polly never married. Helen could be more openly critical of Polly in a way she never could with Annie. Helen lost her temper when Polly told her her favorite coat looked "too shabby" to wear to town. She sometimes became impatient when Polly did not shorten finger-spelling translations of letters. As the years went by, Polly, like Annie, became increasingly possessive of Helen.

In 1946, a fire destroyed Helen and Polly's house at Arcan Ridge in Westport while they were on one of their overseas tours of Italy, France, Greece, and England. "Something broke in Polly when the house burned," a friend wrote. All of Helen's notes that she was putting together on a book about Annie were destroyed. Also burned were diaries, love letters from Peter Fagan to Helen, and John Macy's letters to Annie. Somehow sixty-six-year-old Helen remained remarkably serene.

The house was generously rebuilt by the American Foundation for the Blind. Characteristically stubborn, Helen refused to give up on the book project, which had been nearly three-quarters finished when it was destroyed. She went to work on a new manuscript, starting from scratch, which she titled simply *Teacher*. The book would eventually be published in 1955.

A neighbor and friend who knew Helen later in life commented, "Unlike the majority of the blind, who are apt to fail earlier than those who see, and are even supposed to die earlier in life, Helen Keller, with every year, seemed to grow more vigorous as she continually extended the scope of her work."

In 1955, filmmaker Nancy Hamilton and actress and friend Katherine

Cornell released Helen's film biography, *The Unconquered*, which was renamed *Helen Keller in Her Story*. The film included unusual footage of Helen experiencing a special dance choreographed by Martha Graham. *Helen Keller in Her Story* won an Oscar for best feature-length documentary that year. Two years later, in 1957, *Playhouse 90* presented a television play called *The Miracle Worker*, written by William Gibson. This told of Helen's first meeting with Annie Sullivan. Later, the teleplay was expanded into a full-length drama that opened on Broadway in 1959 and was later made into an Academy Award–winning movie.

On her seventy-fifth birthday, a reporter asked Helen what she planned to do with the remaining years of her life. She told him she would work for the handicapped while she still had breath in her body. She'd also like to study the great philosophers, Plato and Swedenborg, and learn to speak Russian.

At age seventy-seven, she spoke frankly about the great struggles of her life. "No one knows—no one can know—the bitter denials of limitation better than I do. I am not deceived by my situation. It is not true that I am not sad or rebellious; but long ago I determined not to complain. The mortally wounded must strive to live out their days cheerfully for the sake of others." What kept her going, she said, was her work, the solace of friendship, and "an unwavering faith in God's Plan of Good."

While Helen seemed to grow younger and stronger, Polly, intrepid traveler, began to fail. With each passing year she became increasingly possessive of Helen. She fired maids. She refused to allow people to speak to Helen directly, even if they knew manual spelling. She became so obsessed with Helen's appearance that she would not allow uninvited callers in the house if Helen wasn't looking impeccably groomed.

Beginning in 1948, Polly had suffered the first of what would be a series of strokes caused by high blood pressure. In the early spring of 1960, Helen stayed with Polly after she collapsed on the floor of the kitchen. For two and a half hours, Helen hovered over seventy-six-year-old Polly until help arrived. Polly died March 21, 1960, with eighty-year-old Helen at her side.

In 1955 Helen published Teacher, *a biography of Annie Sullivan Macy, and embarked on a forty-thousand-mile, five-month tour of the Far East.*

15.

"Someone Who Liked to Laugh"

I am constantly on the lookout for miracles. The unexpected might happen at any odd moment, and I want to be on the spot.

—Helen Keller, *Midstream*

AFTER POLLY'S DEATH Helen's care went to a new assistant, Winifred (Winnie) Corbally, a bright, warmhearted nurse who had learned manual spelling and enjoyed Helen's company. "Those were the fun years," Corbally wrote. "It was a time of her life when she could have fun. Miss Keller was a rogue. . . . We had oodles of fun. We would go to a hot-dog stand. Polly Thomson would never allow hot dogs in the house. But Miss Helen loved them. 'Don't forget the mustard,' she would say."

One day in the spring of 1960, fourteen-year-old child actress Patty Duke visited Helen Keller at her home in Connecticut. Helen always enjoyed the company of children, perhaps because they were more open and showed less of adults' hesitancy and awkwardness around her. When children spelled words into her hand with small, awkward fingers, she said they were like "the wildflowers of conversation."

Duke was playing the part of young Helen in *The Miracle Worker*, the Broadway play about Helen's early life. The show had opened to rave reviews and would later be turned into an acclaimed movie. Duke and Anne Bancroft, who played Annie, both won Academy Awards for their performances. Duke was the youngest actress ever to receive this award. "I felt transported," Duke said of performing her role as Helen, an experience she described as "almost religious."

Naturally, Duke felt nervous about meeting the world-famous Helen Keller in person. Helen walked regally down the stairs to meet her wearing an impeccable blue dress, pearls, and her favorite red high-heel shoes. Her pale skin shone like alabaster; her very white hair was fine as an angel's.

In June 1960, child actress Patty Duke from The Miracle Worker *shared confidences with Helen during her eightieth birthday party at the Gotham Hotel in New York City. To the left of Helen is Evelyn Seide, who served as one of Helen's last assistants.*

Helen's terrific smile took Duke by surprise. "She was so jolly, like a jolly grandma. I'd expected serious or sweet, but not jolly. Not someone who was so much fun. Not someone who liked to laugh, and about everything, even the fact that we'd come before she'd had a chance to take her bras—rather large bras, I might add—in off the laundry line."

Helen gave her a big hug. They walked outside to the garden, where she was introduced to Helen's enormous dogs. Helen spelled words into Duke's hand "just to be gracious and indulge me because I wanted her to." Most of the time Helen spoke. "Her voice was very hard to understand, like a computer talking," Duke said. "To understand me, she would put her thumb on my lips and her fingers on different vibration points. She didn't miss a thing."

Helen walked arm in arm with Duke, following the garden railing and pointing out lilac bushes, sweet-scented roses, and budding hawthorn. The two companionable ramblers, separated by sixty-six years of age, must have presented a somewhat curious scene to Winnie Corbally, who followed at a respectful distance. Here was a hearing and sighted child who had studied carefully how to appear deaf and blind. And here was a deaf and blind woman who had studied carefully how to appear hearing and sighted.

At one point, Helen paused and told Duke how these strolls in the garden made her feel at one with nature. Then she added in her characteristically disarming way that the other thing she really enjoyed was her evening martini. If the doctor didn't approve, well, that was really too bad. At her age, she told Duke, if she enjoyed a martini, she was going to have one.

Even at eighty Helen continued to do her best to topple her saintly image.

Helen officially retired from public life in 1961. In her last years her medical expenses, household help, finances, and home repairs were taken care of through the generosity and management of the board of the American Foundation for the Blind.

She died June 1, 1968, at Arcan Ridge a few days after a heart attack. She had never feared death. "What is so sweet as to awake from a troubled dream and behold a beloved face smiling upon you?" she once wrote. "I have to believe that such shall be our awakening from earth to heaven."

Winnie Corbally, who sat beside her bed during her last moments, said Helen "drifted off in her sleep. She died gently."

Even in death, people tried to remake Helen to fit the image of the person they wanted her to be.

One of Helen's last requests was to be cremated and to have a Swedenborgian minister perform a simple funeral service for her in Connecticut. However, an elaborate ceremony took place for her at the National Cathedral in Washington, D.C., on June 5, 1968. The Swedenborgian service was canceled. "We never went for the Swedenborg stuff at all," admitted her brother, Phillips.

Helen's family went one step further and tried to erase her embarrassing radical political beliefs as well. Phillips invited his old school chum, U.S. Senator Joseph Lister Hill, a seventy-three-year-old Democrat from Alabama, to read Helen's eulogy. Helen, always a great supporter of racial equality, would have been appalled. Conservative Hill had proudly voted against every piece of civil rights legislation ever introduced to Congress.

A special section of pews had been set aside for the blind with Seeing Eye dogs—something that would have pleased Helen, who always liked almost any kind of dog. A translator stood in the front of the church, deftly transforming every spoken word into sign language, the form of communication that the deaf of Helen's generation had been forbidden to use. Most enjoyable of all for Helen would undoubtedly have been the sightless fifty-member choir from the Perkins School for the Blind. Their young voices soared and echoed through the cathedral accompanied by organ music that rumbled across the floor into the feet of the hearing and deaf, sighted and blind alike.

Epilogue

VIOLENCE AND PEACE, destruction and hope haunted Americans in 1968, the year that Helen Keller died. The country was convulsed by an unpopular war, racial and economic unrest, and the tragic assassination of two important political figures.

No one can know for sure what Helen would have thought about the avalanche of public events and profound cultural changes that cascaded across America that year. One thing is certain. She would have reacted passionately. As she pointed out in *Midstream*, "I like frank debate." The watchwords of her life—promotion of peace, improved race relations, and justice for the poor and disabled—were all topics of intense discussion, protest, and action in 1968. Helen would undoubtedly have been in the thick of it.

In 1968 the United States was deeply involved in a disastrous and unpopular war in Vietnam, a $30 billion-per-year struggle that had begun in 1957 and would not end until 1975 with a total loss of more than 58,000 American lives. In 1968 antiwar and antidraft protest spread across the country.

Throughout her life, Helen Keller had sharp words against militarism, the industrial buildup of arms, and destruction of lives. As early as 1915, she suggested that soldiers defy their leaders, quit fighting, and "put their hands in their pockets and go home"—words which would have sounded surprisingly contemporary in 1968.

The civil rights movement that began in the early 1960s reached a peak of fear and confusion in 1968. On April 4, thirty-nine-year-old African-American civil rights leader Martin Luther King Jr. was assassinated in Memphis. After a stunned nation learned of his death, riots broke out in 168 towns and cities. An estimated fifteen thousand troops were called in to end looting and fires with damage estimates totaling more than $13.3 million. Two months later, on June 6, the day after Helen Keller's funeral

In 1961 Helen met with President John F. Kennedy, who championed many of her favorite causes. Evelyn Seide (center) assisted her on this trip to Washington, D.C.

service, forty-three-year-old Democratic presidential hopeful Robert Kennedy, a civil rights activist determined to end the war in Vietnam, was gunned down in Los Angeles.

Helen would have been both shocked and dismayed. All her life she supported racial equality and the peaceful resolution of conflicts, even when doing so meant going against the opinions of her southern family and friends. The same woman who donated money and public support to the NAACP fifty years earlier—much to her relatives' consternation—also said she most admired "courage, vision, and unyielding determination" in leaders. These were certainly qualities evident both in Martin Luther King Jr. and Robert Kennedy. As Helen once explained to progressive candidate Robert La Follette, she was always on the lookout for leaders who used peaceable methods of settling differences, "as opposed to intolerance, hatred, and violence."

What perhaps would have pleased Helen most about 1968 were the programs for the disabled that had finally begun to flower. Many of these initiatives had taken root during Helen's early years crisscrossing the country for the American Foundation for the Blind, now known as the American Federation for the Blind (AFB). Her pioneering support and tireless efforts to promote awareness of the disabled helped lay the groundwork for a number of pathbreaking new programs and legislation.

For more than five decades she regularly testified before Congress and worldwide blind and deaf organizations to support distribution of cheap or free Braille books in uniform style; scholarships for education and job training; initiation of teacher training programs; and improved disabled access to public transportation.

In 1968, the disabled and the parents of disabled children organized a successful effort to press Congress to pass laws to protect the rights and guarantee job, transportation, and education access for individuals who were blind, deaf, paralyzed or in wheelchairs, mentally ill or mentally handicapped. The movement was inspired by the passage of the Civil Rights Act of 1964, which defined and expanded the guarantees of freedom and equality for men and women, both rich and poor, of all races and ethnic backgrounds.

The disabled who spearheaded these efforts to change laws refused to be considered deviant, incompetent, unhealthy objects of fear who had to depend on welfare and the charity of others. They refused to be treated as second-class citizens excluded from decent jobs, housing, and education. They wanted to choose, to belong, to participate, to have dignity and opportunity—all goals that Helen Keller had struggled toward for herself and others during her lifetime.

The year 1968 was really the beginning of an important shift. Instead of relying on private or local charities to help the disabled, the federal government mandated sweeping new changes for all the states. The 1968 Architectural Barriers Act required federally funded or leased buildings to be barrier-free for people in wheelchairs. Two years later, the 1970 Urban Mass Transportation Act would be passed to make buses and trains accessible to the handicapped. In 1973 the Rehabilitation Act declared that no employer who received federal financial assistance could discriminate against a possible employee with a disability. A major landmark in 1975 would be passage of the Education for All Handicapped Children Act, which was designed to provide all disabled children a free, appropriate education in "the least restrictive environment." This meant that disabled students could enter the public school system with non-disabled students.

None of these laws was perfect. In the years following their passage, many were rewritten and refined. On the eve of the twenty-first century, the basic goal, however, remains the same: "[T]o assure equality of opportunity, full participation, independent living, and economic self-sufficiency" for the disabled.

Many challenges remain. The U. S. Department of Commerce estimates that about nine million Americans of all ages have disabilities so severe that they need personal assistance to carry out everyday activities. As the population becomes older, the number of people with disabilities will grow. People with disabilities experience the highest unemployment rate and the most prevalent levels of welfare. The disabled are more likely than the non-disabled to live in poor housing, attend substandard schools, and be provided with less than adequate transportation and services.

At the same time, much has changed since Helen Keller was a young girl. She would undoubtedly be pleased to discover that today children with disabilities have the right to board a bus and be sent to a school that's best for them. When they grow up they have a broad range of college opportunities. Always a physically active person, Helen would be delighted to find that people with disabilities are recognized for their performance in sports and have been included in the Olympic Games. As a curious and eager user of technology, she would undoubtedly find remarkable the profound impact computers have had on the daily life of the disabled—from how well wheelchairs operate on steep inclines to special telecommunications for the blind and deaf. Technology has also created new jobs for people with disabilities.

Like other disabled people, Helen Keller was much more than her blindness or her deafness. With energy and a sense of humor, she fearlessly went out into the world to travel and work—something that the disabled are being encouraged to do now more than ever. She saw herself first and foremost as a free, self-reliant woman, "a human being with a mind of her own." As she wrote in her 1937 journal while on a trip around the world speaking on behalf of the deaf and blind, "I use my limitations as tools, not as my real self."

If she were alive today, she would expect the disabled to do nothing less.

Helen at age eighty remained a devoted reader.

Chronology

April 14, 1866	Annie Sullivan is born in Agawam, Massachusetts
June 27, 1880	Helen Adams Keller is born in Tuscumbia, Alabama
1880	Annie admitted to Perkins Institution for the Blind, Boston
February 1882	Helen becomes gravely ill; recovers but loses her hearing and sight
March 3, 1887	Annie Sullivan arrives in Tuscumbia to become Helen's teacher
1888	Helen, her mother, and Annie visit the Perkins Institution for the Blind
September 1889	Helen and Annie move to Boston so that Helen can attend Perkins
1890	Helen receives speech lessons from Sarah Fuller of the Horace Mann School for the Deaf
1891	Helen sends Anagnos "The Frost King"
October 1894	Helen enters the Wright-Humason School in New York City
August 19, 1896	Helen's father, Captain Arthur H. Keller, dies; Helen becomes a Swedenborgian
October 1896	Helen moves back to Boston to attend the Cambridge School for Young Ladies
1899	Helen passes Radcliffe preliminary entrance exams
September 1900	Helen enters Radcliffe College
1902–1903	*The Story of My Life* is published in serial form in the *Ladies' Home Journal*, then as a book
June 28, 1904	Helen graduates cum laude from Radcliffe
1904	Helen and Annie purchase farm at Wrentham, Massachusetts

May 2, 1905	Annie marries John Albert Macy
1908	Publication of *The World I Live In*
1909	Helen becomes a socialist and suffragist
1913	Publication of *Out of the Dark*
January 1914	John Albert Macy files for a divorce
1914	Polly Thomson joins Helen's household
1915–1916	Helen meets Peter Fagan and makes plans to marry him; Polly and Annie go to Puerto Rico; Helen goes home to Montgomery
1917	Helen and Annie sell farm at Wrentham; Helen, Annie, and Polly move to Forest Hills, New York
1919	Helen stars in *Deliverance*, a silent movie about her life; Helen begins a tour on the vaudeville circuit
November 20, 1921	Helen's mother, Kate Adams Keller, dies
1923–1924	Helen begins working as a fund-raiser for the American Foundation for the Blind
1927	Publication of *My Religion*
1928	Publication of *Midstream: My Later Life*
August 26, 1932	John Macy dies
October 20, 1936	Annie dies in Forest Hills
1938	Publication of *Helen Keller's Journal: 1936–1937*; sale of house in Forest Hills
1940	Publication of *Let Us Have Faith*
1943	Helen begins hospital visits to blind, deaf, and wounded soldiers
1946	Tours to Greece, England, France, Italy; Helen's home in Westport is destroyed by fire
1948	Tours to Australia, New Zealand, Japan; Polly's first stroke
1951	Tours to South Africa

1952	Tours to Egypt, Lebanon, Syria, Jordan, Israel
1953	Release of documentary on Helen's life, *The Unconquered*
1955	Publication of *Teacher*; tours of India and Japan
1957	Publication of *The Open Door*; first (television) production of *The Miracle Worker*; tour of Scandinavia
March 21, 1960	Polly Thomson dies
1961	Helen suffers first stroke; retires from public life
June 1, 1968	Helen dies

Source Notes

Writer Eudora Welty once said that she hoped her work would help "part a curtain, that invisible shadow that falls between people, the veil of indifference to each other's presence, each other's wonder, each other's human plight." Investigating Helen Keller involved a similar challenge—how to uncover the real human being whose fascinating life has become an American legend.

Most helpful were Helen's numerous books, newspaper and magazine articles, and her journals, especially those published after Annie Sullivan's death. Also valuable was the Hadley School for the Blind's collection of original letters and reminiscences of Helen and Annie. Early reports from the Perkins School for the Blind provided insights into Helen's growing fame. The Alabama State Archives collection of *The North Alabamian* proved helpful in understanding Tuscumbia and Helen's family.

I found especially moving a videotape of Helen and Annie created from rare film footage included in *The Unconquered*. Extensive photos, letters, and memorabilia from the American Foundation for the Blind thoroughly cover the latter part of Helen's career.

Highly recommended books about the senses include: David Howes's *The Varieties of Sensory Experience* and Diane Ackerman's *A Natural History of the Senses.* Walter Percy's *The Message in the Bottle* offers a fascinating examination of how Helen may have acquired language. Thomas D. Cutsforth's *The Blind in School and Society* and Frances A. Koestler's excellent *The Unseen Minority* provide insights into the world of the blind. Lane's and Higgins's numerous books on the deaf experience are most helpful. Wright's personal account of deafness is especially poignant. James Haskins's *Who Are the Handicapped?* and Alan Gartner's *Images of the Disabled, Disabling Images* are among many helpful books investigating laws and rights of the disabled.

Fine women's histories include Carol Blesser's *In Joy and In Sorrow* and Carroll Smith-Rosenberg's *Disorderly Conduct.* Leftwich's, McMillan's, and Griffith's regional histories proved key in understanding Alabama and the South. I found helpful numerous books covering America's history during Helen's eventful lifetime. Among these I would especially recommend Frederick Lewis Allen's *The Big Change,* Meirien and Susan Harries's *The Last Days of Innocence,* and Milton Rugott's *America in the Gilded Age.*

For Further Reading

BOOKS BY HELEN KELLER

The Story of My Life. With Her Letters (1887–1901) and a Supplementary Account of Her Education. New York: Doubleday, 1904.

The World I Live In. New York: The Century Co., 1908.

Midstream: My Later Life. Garden City, N.Y.: Sun Dial Press, 1937.

Helen Keller's Journal: 1936–1937. Garden City, N.Y.: Doubleday, Doran, 1938.

Out of the Dark: Essays, Letters and Addresses on Physical and Social Vision. Garden City, N.Y.: Doubleday, Page, 1913.

Teacher: Anne Sullivan Macy. New York: Doubleday, 1955.

The Open Door. Garden City, N.Y.: Doubleday & Co., 1957.

Optimism, an Essay. New York: Doubleday, 1903.

Light in My Darkness. Revised and edited by Ray Silverman. West Chester,
     Penn.: Chrysalis Books, 1994.

The Song of the Stone Wall. London: Hodder & Stoughton, 1910.

Helen Keller in Scotland. London: Methuen, 1933.

Let Us Have Faith. New York: Doubleday, Doran, 1940.

Peace at Eventide. London: Methuen, 1932.

BOOKS ABOUT HELEN KELLER AND ANNIE SULLIVAN MACY

Braddy, Nella (Henney). *Anne Sullivan Macy: The Story Behind Helen Keller*.
     Garden City, N.Y.: Doubleday, Doran, 1933.

Carberg, Michael C., ed. *A Helen Keller Scrapbook* (unpublished). Winnetka,
     Ill.: Hadley School for the Blind, 1972.

Harrity, Richard, and Ralph G. Martin. *The Three Lives of Helen Keller*.
     New York: Doubleday, 1962.

Herrmann, Dorothy. *Helen Keller: A Life*. New York: Alfred A. Knopf, 1998.

Lash, Joseph P. *Helen and Teacher*. New York: Delacorte Press, 1980.

Van Wyck, Brooks. *Helen Keller: Sketch for a Portrait*. New York: E. P. Dutton,
     1956.

Volta Bureau, *Helen Keller Souvenir*, no. 2 (1892–1899). Washington, D.C.:1899.

PLAYS ABOUT HELEN KELLER

Duke, Patty. *Call Me Anna*. New York: Bantam Books, 1987.

Gibson, William. *The Miracle Worker: A Play for Television*. New York:
     Alfred A. Knopf, 1957.

———. *Monday After the Miracle: A Play in Three Acts*. New York: Dramatists
Play Service, 1983.

FILMS ABOUT HELEN KELLER

Helen Keller (videotape). American Women of Achievement Series, Schlessinger,1995.

Helen Keller. Films for the Humanities, 1989.

Helen Keller (videotape). Nest Entertainment, (animated) 1996.

Helen Keller and Her Teacher (videotape). CRM/McGraw-Hill, 1970.

Helen Keller: Separate Views (videotape). Master Vision, 1982.

The Miracle Worker. Playfilm Productions, United Artists, 1962.

The Unconquered. 1953. Produced by Nancy Hamilton: Reissued on videotape as *Helen Keller: In Her Story.* American Federation of the Blind, 1955.

WEB SITE ABOUT HELEN KELLER

American Federation of the Blind, Helen Keller Archival Collection (photos): http://www.afb.org/afb

BOOK ABOUT LANGUAGE

Percy, Walker. *The Message in the Bottle.* New York: Farrar, Straus & Giroux, 1975.

BOOKS ABOUT AMERICA DURING HELEN KELLER'S LIFETIME

Ali, Tariq, and Susan Watkins. *1968: Marching in the Streets.* New York: Free Press, 1998.

Allen, Frederick Lewis. *The Big Change: America Transforms Itself, 1900–1950.* New York: Harper and Row, 1952.

Bowen, Ezra, ed. *This Fabulous Century, 1879–1900.* New York: Time-Life Books, 1970.

Cashman, Sean Dennis. *America in the Gilded Age.* New York: New York University Press, 1984.

Ginger, Ray. *Age of Excess.* New York: Macmillan, 1965.

Harries, Meirien, and Susie Harries. *The Last Days of Innocence: America At War, 1917–1918.* New York: Random House, 1997.

Kaiser, Charles. *1968 In America.* New York: Grove Press, 1988.

Maddow, Ben. *A Sunday Between Wars: The Course of American Life from 1865–1917.* New York: W. W. Norton, 1979.

Rugoff, Milton. *America's Gilded Age 1850–1890.* New York: Henry Holt, 1989.

BOOKS ABOUT ALABAMA, THE SOUTH, AND RECONSTRUCTION

Cash, W. F. *The Mind of the South.* New York: Alfred A. Knopf, 1941.

Couch, Robert Hill. *Out of Silence and Darkness: The History of the Alabama Institute for Deaf and Blind.* Troy, Ala.: Troy State University Press, 1983.

Griffith, Lucille. *Alabama: A Documentary History to 1900.* Atlanta: University of Alabama Press, 1968.

Leftwich, Nina. *Two Hundred Years at Muscle Shoals*. Tuscumbia, Ala.: Multigraphic Advertising Co., 1935.

McMillan, Malcolm C. *The Alabama Confederate Reader*. Atlanta: University of Alabama Press, 1963.

Peirce, Neal R. *The Deep South States of America*. New York: W. W. Norton, 1972.

Weiner, Jonathon M. *The Social Origins of the New South: Alabama, 1860–1885*. Baton Rouge: Louisiana State University Press, 1978.

Books About History of Women, South and North

Bernhard, Virginia. *Southern Women: Histories and Identities*. Columbia, Mo.: University of Missouri Press, 1992.

Blesser, Carol, ed. *In Joy and In Sorrow: Women, Family, and Marriage in the Victorian South (1830–1900)*. New York: Oxford University Press, 1991.

Lerner, Gerda. *The Female Experience*. Indianapolis: Bobbs-Merrill, 1977.

O'Neill, William. *Everyone Was Brave: The Rise of Feminism in America*. Chicago: Quadrangle Books, 1969.

Smith-Rosenberg, Carroll. *Disorderly Conduct: Visions of Gender in Victorian America*. New York: Alfred A. Knopf, 1985.

Books About Laura Bridgman

Dickens, Charles. *American Notes, 1842: The Works of Charles Dickens*, vol. 14, National Library Editions. New York: Bigelow, Brown, undated.

Gitter, Ellisabeth. "Deaf-Mutes and Heroines in the Victorian Era," in *Victorian Literature and Culture*, vol. 20, pp. 179–97. New York: AMS Press, 1992.

Books About the Senses

Ackerman, Diane. *A Natural History of the Senses*. New York: Vintage Books, 1991.

Howes, David. *The Varieties of Sensory Experience*. Toronto: University of Toronto Press, 1991.

LeGueru, Annich. *Scent: The Mysterious and Essential Powers of Smell*. New York: Random House, 1992.

Montagu, Ashley. *Touching: The Human Significance of the Skin*. New York: Harper and Row, 1971.

Rivlin, Robert, and Karen Gravelle. *Deciphering the Senses*. New York: Simon & Schuster, 1984.

BOOKS ABOUT DEAFNESS, BLINDNESS, AND DISABILITY

Cutsforth, Thomas D. *The Blind in School and Society*. New York: American Foundation for the Blind, 1932.

Gartner, Alan, ed. *Images of the Disabled, Disabling Images*. New York: Praeger, 1987.

Harrison, Maureen, ed. *The Americans with Disabilities Act Handbook*. Beverly Hills, Calif.: Excellent Books, 1992.

Haskins, James. *Who Are the Handicapped?* Garden City, N.Y.: Doubleday, 1978.

Higgins, Paul Cole. "The Deaf Community: Identity and Interaction in a Hearing World." Ph.D. dissertation, Dept. of Sociology, Northwestern University, Evanston, Ill., 1977.

———. *Making Disability*. Springfield, Ill.: Charles C. Thomas, 1992.

———. *Outsiders in a Hearing World*. Beverly Hills, Calif.: Sage Publications, 1980.

Koestler, Frances A. *The Unseen Minority: Social History of Blindness In America*. New York: David McKay Co., 1976.

Lane, Harlan, ed. *The Deaf Experience*. Cambridge: Harvard University Press, 1984.

———. *The Mask of Benevolence: Disabling the Deaf Community*. New York: Alfred A. Knopf, 1992.

———. *When the Mind Hears: History of Deafness*. New York: Random House, 1984.

Ross, Ishbel. *Journey into Light: The Story of Education of the Blind*. New York: Appleton-Century-Crofts, 1950.

Sacks, Oliver. *Seeing Voices: A Journey into the World of the Deaf*. Berkeley, Calif.: University of California Press, 1989.

U.S. Census Bureau, *Statistical Abstract of the United States: 1999*, 119 Edition, Washington, D.C.: U.S. Census Bureau, 1999.

West, Paul. *Words for a Deaf Daughter*. New York: Harper and Row, 1968.

Wright, David. *Deafness: A Personal Account*. New York: Stein & Day, 1969.

———. *Monologue of a Deaf Man*. London: A. Deutsch, 1958.

Index

Page numbers in *italic* refer to illustrations.

Academy Award, 147, 150
Adams (grandmother), 21
African-Americans, 12–14, 115, 118, 127, 134–35
Alabama Institute for the Deaf and Blind, 22, *22*
Alexander, William, 90
Allen, Frederick Lewis, 116
American Federation for the Blind, 139–42, 146, 151, 154
American Notes (Dickens), 27
Anagnos, Michael, 30–31, 49–50, 58, *59*
    "Frost King" scandal and, 59–62
"Apology for Going to College, An," 85
Arcan Ridge, 143, 146, 151
Architectural Barriers Act of 1968, 155
"Autumn Leaves," 59

Bancroft, Anne, 150
Bell, Alexander Melville, *89*
Bell, Dr. Alexander Graham, 2, *29*, 50, 51, 67–68, *69*, 73, *89*, *90*
    on Helen and love, 89–90
    meets the Kellers, 28–30
    work of, 29–30, *30*
Birdie and his Fairy Friends (Canby), 60, 62
Birth control, 119
Blackstone, Sir William, 25
Boston Globe, 124
Braddy, Nella Henney, 141
Braille, 40–41, 43, 88, 105
Bridgman, Laura, 27, *28*, 31, 32, 44, *53*
    Helen and, 52–53
Brooklyn Eagle, 118
Burroughs, John, 70

Call, The, 119
Cambridge School for Young Ladies, 75–80
Canby, Margaret T., 60, 62
Capitalism, 114–19, 140
Carlyle, Thomas, 52
Carnegie, Andrew, 110
Century, 99
Chamberlin, Ed (Uncle Ed), 80, 82

"Chant of Darkness, A," 7
Chaplin, Charlie, 132
Child labor, 114–16
Chisolm, Dr. Julian John, 28
Civil rights, 152–54
Civil Rights Act of 1964, 155
Civil War, 12–14
Cleveland, Grover, 2, 51
Cohan, George M., 127
Commentaries (Blackstone), 25
Coolidge, Calvin, *3*
Copeland, Charles Townsend, 88, 91
Corbally, Winifred, 149, 151, 152
Cornell, Katherine, 146–47

Darwin, Charles, 48, 49
Davidson, Jo, 145
Debs, Eugene V., 117, 128, 137
Deliverance, 129–34
Democratic Vistas (Whitman), 48
Derby, Caroline, 69–70
Dickens, Charles, 25, 27, 52
Disabled persons, programs for, 154–56
Duke, Patty, 149–51, *150*

Edison, Thomas, 47, 110
Education for All Handicapped Children Act of 1975, 155
Elliott, Maude Howe, 110

Fagan, Peter, 122–26, 146
Fairbanks, Douglas, 132
Fairy tales, 58, 59
Family Limitation (Sanger), 119
Fern Quarry, 62–63
Folk cures, 17
Freed slaves, 12–14
French Legion of Honor, 2
"Frost King, The," 58–62, 67
Fuller, Sarah, 55

George, H. Maria, 66
Gibson, William, 147
Gilman, Arthur, 76, 79, 80
Goldman, Emma, 128
Goodson Gazette, The, 60
Graham, Martha, 147
Great Depression, 142

Haas, Herbert, 142
Hale, Dr. Edward Everett, 50
Hamilton, Nancy, 146
Haywood, "Big" Bill, 128
"Helen Keller As She Really Is," 94
Helen Keller Day, 98
Helen Keller in Her Story, 147
Helen Keller Souvenir, 67
Henney, Nella Braddy, 125, 144
Hill, Lister, 152
Hitz, John, 63, 73, 75, 82, *89*, 95, 98, 102
Holmes, Dr. Oliver Wendell, 56
Hooper, Jami, 143
Hopkins, Sophia C., 60, 79
Household, The, 65–66
Howe, Dr. Samuel Gridley, 27, 32, 44
Humason, Dr. Thomas, 69, 70
Hunter, Robert, 114
Hutton, Eleanor, 79, 83
Hutton, Lawrence, 70

Immigration, 48
Industrial Workers of the World (IWW), 126, 128–29
Intercollegiate Socialist Society, 128
Irwin, Robert, 139
Ivy Green, 11, *11*, *20*, *21*, 33, *35*, *37*, *42*

Japan, 143–44, 145

Keith, Merton S., 83
Keller, Captain Arthur B., 9–15, *9*, 27
    Civil War and, 12
    death of, 72–73
    described, 11–12
    financial difficulties of, 56, 57, 72
    "Frost King" scandal and, 61
    on Helen's affliction, 18
    Helen's fame and, 50–51
    racism of, 13–14
    Sullivan and, 33, 44, 79
Keller, Evaline (Aunt Ev), 22, 28
Keller, Frank, 41
Keller, Helen:
    autobiography of, 90–92
    Bell and, 28–30, 50, 51, 67–68

benefactors of, 67, 69, 70, 72, 80, 95, 99, 110, 142, 151
birth of, 9–10
Braille and, *38*, 40–41, 43, 88, 105, *157*
Bridgman and, 52–53
as a celebrity, 44, 49–51, 58–59, 67, 98, 103–104
charitable causes and, 103–105, 139–46, 154–56
childhood of, *i, ii*, 18–25, *26, 38, 46, 52, 54, 57, 59, 64, 68, 69, 74*
college preparation, 65, 75–80
connection with her audience, 112–19, 135
death of, 151–52
death of parents, 72–73, 137
described:
    as a baby, 10
    at Cambridge, 78
    with glass eyes, 106
    on the lecture circuit, 113
    at Perkins, 67
discovers language, 36–37, 49, 135–36
Fagan and, 122–26
film biography, 146–47
finances of, 72, 90, 95, 99, 103, 106, 107, 110, 114, 129, 134
as fund raiser, 103–105
health of, 79–80, 88
in Hollywood, 129–34, *132, 133*
identity struggles, 81, 82–83, 88, 104
independence of, 88, 143
lecture tours of, 110–21
letters by, *50*, 57–58
loses hearing and vision, 2, 15, 17–18
Macy and, 91–95, *93, 100*
memory of, 92
as a "miracle," 2, 98
the ocean and, 7–9
perceptiveness of, 45
at the Perkins Institution, 1–2, 49–62, *52*, 67
pets of, 19, *26*, 36, 41–42, *46*, 56, *57, 84, 87, 87, 100*, 103, *103*, 128, 129, *138*
photographs of, *3, 6, 89, 90, 103, 107, 112, 120, 125, 145, 148, 150, 154*
plagiarism scandal, 58–63, 67

poem dedicated to, 95
politics and, 106, 116–22, 126–27, 135, 140–41, 144–45
posters of, *111, 130*
at Radcliffe, 84–98, *84, 87, 90, 96*
certificate of admission to, *86*
reading and, *38*, 41, *157*
religion of, 73, 82, 137, 141, 152
romance and, 66–67, 89–90, 122–26
sensory experiences, 99–102
social reform and, 114–22, 128–29, 135, 153–56
speech training, 69–70, 75, 104, 106, 109–10
Sullivan and, *ii, 68, 69, 74, 87, 89, 93, 100, 108, 111, 123, 138*
teacher of, *see* Sullivan, Annie
Thompson and, *132, 138, 143, 144*
Twain and, 70–72
uncertainty about the future, 95, 97, 98–99
use of manual alphabet, *see* Manual alphabet
on the vaudeville circuit, 135–39, *136*
as young woman, 67, 78, 81–83
as zealous learner, 40–45
Keller, James, 11, 33
Keller, Kate Adams, 9–11, *9*, 27, 99, *133*
death of, 137
described, 10
health of Helen and, 79–80
on Helen's affliction, 18
marriage of, 10–11
marriage of Helen and, 124–26
prudishness of, 67, 126
Sullivan and, 33, 45
Keller, Mildred, 7, 41–43, 57, *77*, 82, 125
at Cambridge School, 76–80
fire at home of, 126
Keller, Phillips, 56, *133*, 152
Keller, Sarah, 11
Keller, Simpson, 11
Keller family, *9*, 11, 15, 18–19, 56, 72, *77*, 118, 122, 126, *133*, 152
meets Bell, 28–30

Keller's Landing, 39–40
Kennedy, John F., 2, *154*
Kennedy, Robert, 153–54
King, Martin Luther, Jr., 153, 154
Ku Klux Klan, 13, 137

Ladies Home Journal, 90, 95, 104
La Follette, Robert, 140, *154*
Lee, General Robert E., 12
Little House, 10, *10*, 11, *11, 16*, 35–36, *36*
Louisiana Purchase Exposition, 98
"Ludlow Massacre," 115
Lynd, Helen, 23
Lynd, Robert, 23
Lyon, Edmund, *68*

McClure's Magazine, 85
Macy, John Albert, 91–95, *91, 93, 100*, 124, 146
marriage of, 99, 102–103, 105–107, 119
Maddow, Ben, 117
Manual alphabet, 1–2, 19, 30, 70, 94
diagram of, *4*
Bell on, 28
at Radcliffe, 86, 87–88
Sullivan using, 34, 36–37, 87, 88
Marx, Karl, 93, 116
Massachusetts Commission for the Blind, 104
Mentor, The, 60
Middletown (Lynd and Lynd), 23
Midstream: My Later Life (Keller), 97, 131, 141, 149, 153
Migel, "Major" Moses Charles, 142
Miracle Worker, The, 147, 149–50
Mitchell, S. Weir, 65
"My Future As I *See* It," 95
My Religion (Keller), 73, 141

National Association for the Advancement of Colored People (NAACP), 127
National Cathedral, 142–43, 152
"Natural selection," 48
Nazis, 144
1968, 153–55
North Alabamian, The, 11, 13–14, *14*, 18, 28
O'Neill, William, 97
Ophthalmia neonatorum, 104–105
Out of the Dark (Keller), 118–19

Pacifism, 117–18, 121–22, 127, 128–29, 144–45, 153
Perkins Institution for the Blind, *1*, 23, 27, 30, 32, 104, 152
    Helen at, 1–2, 49–62, 67
Pickford, Mary, 132
Playhouse 90, 147
Poverty, *24*, 114–16, 118, 140
Poverty (Hunter), 114
Prate, Polly, *68*
Pratt-Smoots Bill, 141
Prejudice:
    against the blind and deaf, 23–25
    racial, 12–14, 134–35
Presidential Medal of Freedom, 2
Proper young ladies, 65–66

Radcliffe College, 75, 84–88
    graduation from, 96–98
    heavy workload at, 88
    other young women at, 86–87
    preparation for, 75–80
Reconstruction, 12, 13
Red Farm, 80, *80*, 82–83
Rehabilitation Act of 1973, 155
"Remarks on Housekeeping," 65–66
Rhoen, Nicholas C., 143
Robbins, Elizabeth, *54*
Rockefeller, John D., 115
Rogers, Henry Huddleston, 70, 72, 99
Romania, Queen of, 99
Roosevelt, Eleanor, 2
Roosevelt, Franklin D., 140
Russian Revolution, 128, 135

Sandberg, Carl, 5
Sanger, Margaret, 119
Science Monthly, 50
Seeing Eye dogs, 152
Seide, Evelyn, 150, *154*
Selma Journal, 127
Sharecroppers, 13, 14
Socialism, 106, 117–19, 122, 124, 128–29, 135
"Song of the Stone Wall," 102–103
Spanish-American War, 81
Spaulding, John S., 95
Stedman, Clarence, 70
Stokes, Rose Pastor, 128
Stormfield, 72
Story of My Life, The (Keller), 7, 27, 39, 55

writing of, 90–92
Strikes, 115, 116, 128, 134
Stringer, Tommy, *54*, 104
"Striving," 48–49
Sullivan, Annie:
    changed by Helen, 40
    death of, 142–43
    described, 31–32, 56–57, 93–94, 118
    early lessons, 34–37
    Fagan and, 124
    "Frost King" scandal and, 60–63
    health of, 94, 97, 107, 122, 128, 137, 141–42
    Helen's name for, 37
    lecture tour and, 110–14
    Macy and, 93–95, 99, 102–103, 105–107
    making enemies, 58, 75, 79
    manual alphabet and, 34, 36–39
    meets Helen, 33–34, 147
    mood changes of, 44–45, 51, 80–81, 101, 102, 107, 140
    at Perkins Institution, 32
    photographs of, *ii, 31, 43, 68, 69, 74, 87, 89, 93, 100, 108, 111, 123, 138*
    poor eyesight of, 32, 57, 88, 94, 137, 139, 141
    possessiveness of, 45, 51, 56–57, 67
    religion and, 73
    separated from Helen, 57–58, 79–80
    spending habits of, 51–52, 126
    at the Tewksbury poorhouse, 31
    uncertainty about the future, 95, 97
Swedenborgianism, 73, 82, 89, 147, 152

Talcott, Carolyn, 68–69
"Talking glove," 51
Teacher (Keller), 75, 146
Thomas, Edith, *52, 54*
Thomson, Polly, 119, 122, 126–29, *132,* 137, *138,* 142–47, *143,* 149
    after Sullivan's death, 143–47
    death of, 147

described, 145–46
Tolstoy, Leo, 93
Tuscumbia, Alabama, 9–15, *15,* 33, *40,* 44, 56, 69
Twain, Mark, 2, 70–72, *71*
Tyson, Warren, 122

Unconquered, The, 146–47
Unions, 115
Urban Mass Transportation Act of 1968, 155

Victorian era:
    blind-deaf in, 25, 102
    1890s, 47–49
    venereal disease in, 104–105
    women in, 65–66, 97
Virginia Institution for the Education of the Deaf and Dumb, 60
Volta Bureau, 67
Volta Review, 67

Wade, William, 55, 69
War Between the States, 12–14
Washington, Martha, 19–20
Wells, H. G., 93
White, Charles A., 106, 110, 112
Whitman, Walt, 48, 67, 82
Whittier, John Greenleaf, 56
Willard, Frances E., 66
Wilson, Woodrow, 122, 127
Women's Education and Industrial Union, 104
Women's Peace Party, 117
Women's suffrage, 106, 119, 134
World Council for the Blind, 141
World I Live In, The (Keller), 7, 65, 99–102, 109, 139
World's Columbian Exposition of 1893, 67–68
World War I, 117, 121–22, 127
    aftermath of, 134–35
World War II, 144–45
Wrentham farm, 95, 99, *100,* 103, 105–106, 121, 127–28
Wright, David, 5, 62
Wright, John D., 69, 70
Wright-Humason School, 69–70, 72, 75

Youth's Companion, 63, 91, 99

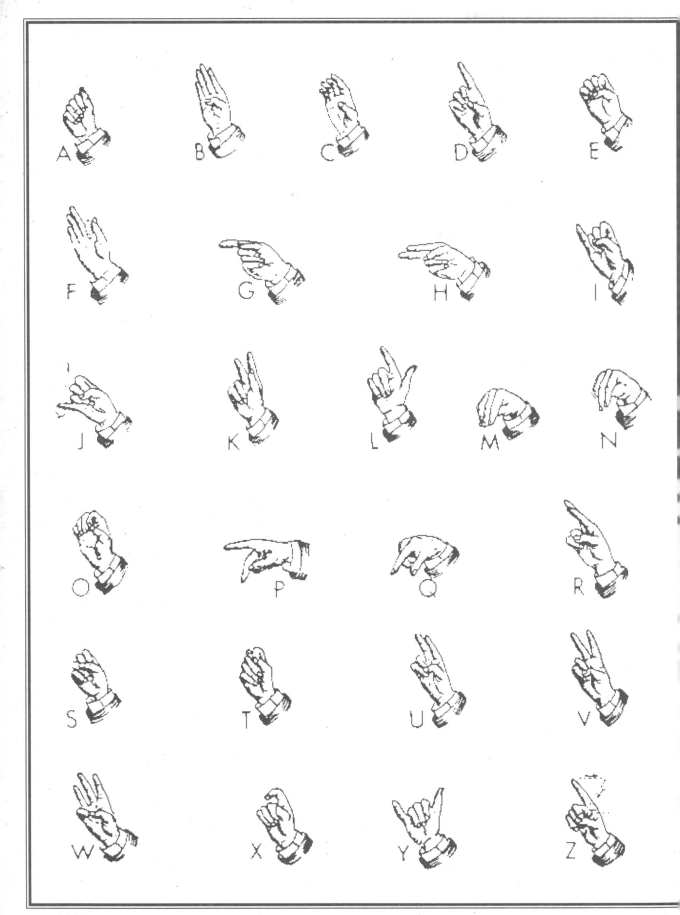